MW00617403

I
BELIEVE

BRENDA O'BRIEN

A SOUTHERN GIRL'S STORY OF SURVIVAL

I BELIEVE

For information about this title or to order other books and/or electronic media, contact the publisher:

Brenda O'Brien
https://www.brendaobrienauthor.com/
BrendaIbelieve@gmail.com

ISBNs:
978-1-0879631-6-7 (print)
979-8-9854576-1-2 (eBook)

Printed in the United States of America

Cover and Interior design: 1106 Design

To My Three Miracles,
Jack, Brett, and Steven

Table of Contents

Preface

This book about my life, written when I was 80, is full of darkness. I got through it all by believing in God and seeing the light. I learned along the way that life is good if you have music and positive vibes. Life will always offer you a choice to see things with light and love. I tried to reach out for positive things and to believe in myself. This practice has guided me through rough times.

My attitude toward life, and the inspiration for the title of this book, can be found in the song "I Believe," by Frankie Laine, which my classmates and I sang at high school graduation:

I believe for every drop of rain that falls
A flower grows

I believe that somewhere in the darkest night
A candle glows

I believe for everyone who goes astray
Someone will come to show the way

I believe. I believe

I believe above the storm the smallest prayer
Will still be heard

I believe that someone in the great somewhere
Hears every word

Every time I hear a newborn baby cry or touch a leaf or see the sky
Then I know why I believe

Every time I hear a newborn baby cry or touch a leaf or see the sky
Then I know why I believe

This song, which stayed with me my whole life, ignited the good fire in me and gave me a lot of strength during my journey. What follows is my story.

Chapter 1

The Beginning

I was born in Memphis, Tennessee, on September 8, 1940—the day of celebration for the birth of the Virgin Mary. My mother Clemmye would later tell me that I was born on the Virgin Mary's birthday. I was a ten-pounder.

I was named after Brenda Starr, the famous comic-book character. I kind of like that. My middle name is Lou, perhaps after my father's father, Louis. It's not my favorite name. But people closest to me liked "Brenda Lou," so I heard that name my whole life.

My mother told me that, when I was young, I would wrap my hand around her little finger, very, very tight. It happened to be the finger she'd caught in a train door and broken a few years before I was born. It was thus a bit crooked. I always remembered that story. I squeezed my mom's broken finger, and I was so huge and strong that I could do it very tight.

I grew up in West Memphis, Arkansas, a tiny town on the western bank of the Mississippi River, opposite Memphis, Tennessee. West Memphis was known as the "Wonder City," since it grew out of river marshes and swamps into a bustling town dominated by the cotton and lumber industries. My mother Clemmye and my father, Morris

Berger, were prominent citizens and businesspeople in West Memphis, beginning in the 1940s.

My father, Morris, was the second child of Louis and Sarah Berger, who were born in Russia on July 4, 1884 and in March 1891, respectively. Louis and Sarah were Jews who emigrated to the United States in the early twentieth century. Louis, who was known as Louie, was medium-built and had blue eyes and jet-black hair. Sarah was short, five feet three inches, but was known as "Big Mama" because of her big boobs.

The 1910 federal census indicates that they lived in New York City, but by 1911 they had moved to Harrisburg, Arkansas, twenty miles south of Jonesboro, where my father, Morris, was born on January 7, 1911. Louie and Big Mama had a dry goods store in Harrisburg, where my father worked as a boy, before he became a traveling shoe salesman. Daddy was a free spirit.

My mother was born on September 17, 1912, in the tiny town of Birdie, Mississippi, about sixty miles south of Memphis. She was the youngest child of John William Mullenix and Dona Bell Coggins, both children of Mississippi farmers. John and Dona had six children: John Williams Jr., Erskin, Edgar, Opal, Florene, and my mother, Clemmye Cleo.

I never met my grandmother Dona, but I heard that she was soft spoken, of English descent, and beautiful. She died of breast cancer at an early age in Texas and was buried there. Mother was the only one out of six children, the baby of the family, who was with my grandmother Dona when she died. She buried my grandmother all alone.

Before Mother married Daddy, she went to nursing school with my Aunt Florene and knew enough to care for my grandmother. My grandfather used to say that my grandmother Dona was the only decent thing that came out of Mississippi. He had bad feelings toward Mississippi, but I didn't inherit them. I love so many areas of the Delta, and Mississippi has some beautiful towns and homes.

One story my mother told about her childhood was that her father would sometimes drive her to school in a Model T Ford, and when the tires deflated, they would fill them with cotton. She also said my grandfather had to serve a little time in prison, but I don't know the details. I just know that my father, Morris, did not respect him.

Mother and Daddy met at a county fair in Jonesboro, Arkansas. Mother was visiting her sister Florene. Mother was sitting on a Ferris wheel when, out of nowhere, Morris sat down next to her. My mother later told me about her first meeting with Daddy's family. They were orthodox Jews. They had special soap for dishes and ate only certain foods. My Mother, a Methodist from rural Mississippi, had to make quite an adjustment that day.

Daddy and Mother were married on June 10, 1931, at Frys Mill, Arkansas, a tiny town about halfway between Jonesboro and Memphis. They were a handsome couple. My father sported a pencil moustache and typically wore a bow tie and jacket, gabardine pants, silk socks, and fashionable shoes. Mother was only five feet tall but was a stunner with crystal-blue eyes, dark auburn hair, and stylish clothes. Mother told me that on her first night together, she was shocked to see Daddy wearing a hernia harness, which looked like a giant diaper. She also told me that she and Daddy had sex only three times—one for each child. (I am not sure that is true.)

Daddy and Mother lived many places before they settled down in West Memphis. One was Longview, Texas, which Daddy thought was a good location for his travels as a salesman. My brother Louis Jack and my sister Donna Sue were born in Longview. Donna Sue died at the age of four months from acute acidosis after drinking sour milk on a train trip. She and my mother were returning from a visit to my father at his Army base.

I hope when I get to heaven, I will meet my sister Donna Sue; she has always been my guardian angel. Although I never knew her, I feel she was the only one there watching over me. It has always

Mother and Daddy soon after their marriage

been a good feeling. Everyone needs someone. I knew that God was out there somewhere every day, but still, a backup is always good. Her death was probably the beginning of my father's drinking. But I don't know for sure.

From Texas my parents moved to Memphis sometime in the late 1930s. By this time, Daddy's father had died, and Big Mama had moved to Memphis to live with her sister Rose after selling the family dry goods store in Jonesboro. Daddy got one third of the sale, which was the money he would later use to set himself up in business. Daddy, Mother, and my brother lived in Memphis until 1940, the year I was born, when the family moved across the river to West Memphis, which then had a population of 3,000.

The first building Daddy purchased was our dry goods store. It was the prime property in West Memphis, sitting on Eighth Street and Broadway, in the heart of the Black business district. We lived in the dry goods store as well, at least at first. A lot of the merchandise Daddy got at a literal fire sale from another dry goods store that had caught on fire. He selected the merchandise that was salvageable and that he wanted to sell in his store.

I almost died in that dry goods store soon after I was born. My parents put me to sleep on a pile of new Big John blue overalls folded in stacks on a long walnut table in the store. I was allergic to the dye in the blue jeans, and began choking and turning blue, like the jeans, when my throat closed. Mother rushed me across the street to Dr. Hamilton's office, and then she drove me to the Methodist hospital in Memphis, where I'd been born a few days earlier. I know that Mother was traumatized since she had lost Donna Sue at such a young age. But I survived, and I can tell you right off the bat that was just the beginning of my survival mode.

Me in sombrero in the yard behind the dry goods store

Daddy hooked up a speaker system inside and outside the store tuned to country music to draw in customers. But it was great for me too, since my lullaby as an infant was "You Are My Sunshine," sung by yodeling cowboy Gene Autry, a song that still makes me smile.

These childhood sounds left an impression in my heart and soul, a very deep love of the beat or rhythm of certain music.

Black people in West Memphis shopped around Eighth and Broadway and lived on the streets south of Broadway. They often worked for White people—picking cotton, working in lumber mills and yards, serving as maids. They worked for a White boss and then spent many of their very few hard-earned dollars buying from the merchants on the part of Broadway where our dry goods store was.

Around 90% of our customers were Black. In the daytime, customers would sit on the bright red benches in front of our store and just fan and stay in the shade. As I got older, sometimes I would sit on a red bench and watch the world of Black people around me. Babies were everywhere sucking on their mother's breast, or hopping along, play-pretending.

On the corner was a vendor selling hot tamales, which people could eat faster than he could fill up his steaming home-made cart. Next door to the dry goods store was an appliance store, and across the street were two vacant lots owned by my uncle and Dr. Hamilton's office.

Nearby was a market owned by the Lums, a Chinese family. And further down was a mixture of small-town stores owned by Jewish families, Lebanese families, and families of other nationalities, all filled with food and merchandise to meet the needs mainly of the Black people in the area. I grew up in a Black world where non-Black merchants benefited from selling their goods.

At night and especially on the weekends, Eighth Street near Broadway became a wild place. Many of the old houses and shacks had back-room or under-the-table gambling, and prostitution was rampant. So, too, was violence: knives seemed to be the weapon of choice if an argument broke out. In March 1941, when I was six months old, the Memphis *Commercial Appeal* reported that "a Negro vice boom town has sprung up on Eighth Street of West Memphis to prey on hundreds of Memphis Negroes lured there by a bait of dice, whiskey, and women." Very few White people went to this part of town, except for the sheriff, Bud Holland, who had his hand out at the back door to get his cut, or else he would shut it down.

Music was deep in Black people's bones. Music was their survival mode. The night air was constantly filled with sound from Honky Tonks and blues music, the medicine that people took in every night. The *Encyclopedia of Arkansas History & Culture* says that "in the 1930s, '40s and '50s, Eighth Street was often called Beale Street West, reflecting a music and nightlife scene to equal that in Memphis." So true. There was a rhythm in the night air that no White person could ever comprehend, much less impersonate—not even Elvis. For me, it seemed like heaven. My childhood started out in the very heart and beating pulse of Black town. That experience is still with me.

West of the railroad tracks is where most White people—the middle- and upper-class ones—lived. Broadway, on the west end of town, was filled with nicer shops, banks, restaurants, car dealerships, and drug stores that served only the White people of the town and surrounding communities. Missouri Street, which ran north and south, perpendicular to Broadway, was the gateway to the White neighborhoods. It was dotted with church after church, including the Methodist church I attended. Neither the stores nor the churches on the west end were open to Black people, however. The only reason for being on that side of town was to serve the Whites.

It is strange when you think about it. The White people stayed away from the Black areas because they were afraid and not welcomed.

The only Whites in their area were armed and on the take. The Black people stayed away from the White areas because they were afraid and not welcomed, except when they went there to serve White people.

I grew up hearing tale after tale, and reminders to be careful, about the Ku Klux Klan lurking out in the shadows. My mother's father John was the owner of a farm near Clarksdale, Mississippi. Black sharecropper families worked his land. He got a good deal on some land in Texas, decided to move there, and persuaded some of the Black families to move with him. In Texas, the locals didn't want Black people in their community. So, one night, a group of the Ku Klux Klan marched to the doorstep of his new home and threatened to burn it down along with the other buildings unless he folded up his operation and left the state.

Mother's father listened to the masked KKK leader's threats and replied, "Frank, is that you?" He recognized the voice. It belonged to his banker. "I know you don't want to torch my buildings," he continued. "If you do that, how will I repay you?" And so, the KKK made threats that night but did not follow through. Still, John knew that he couldn't stay. He poured some oil down a well and had an engineer come to declare that there was petroleum under his land. He then sold the land and high-tailed it back to Mississippi.

When I was three or four years old, my parents bought a little house on Pine Street on the west end. Maybe "tiny" would describe it better. It was truly an adorable white doll house with green shutters. I now lived on the "right" side of the tracks, as the saying goes. I believe in my heart that the "right" side of the tracks is your own decision about what you think is right or wrong, and what makes you happy. Anyway, I was always bouncing from the right side to the wrong side, and there was really no right or wrong in my mind.

My brother Louis Jack and me at the Pine Street home

Mother bought an apartment complex and the adjacent lots across the street from our home on Pine Street from her brother, JW. He was an inventor who developed patents for refrigerators. He moved to Yazoo City, Mississippi, around 1943, after he sold the apartments to Mother. His wife was jealous of my mother. Just as my parents did with Donna Sue, JW and his wife named their daughter after my grandmother Dona. Her name was Donna Kay.

I shared my first room with my brother Louis Jack. Later I had a twin bed in my mother's room. I never remember Daddy being in that room, ever. Why the twin beds? I later learned that from about the Civil War until the 1950s, twin beds were seen as a healthier option for married couples. I remember Lucille Ball's show, *I Love Lucy*—they had only twin beds. It was said that twin beds were still the ideal sleeping arrangement for a married couple while they were filming the show. My, how times have changed!

I had to take a nap every afternoon. I never wanted to, but Mother had a magic way of putting me to sleep. She would rub my eyes and sing, *"Go to sleep/my Brenda Lou/'cause Mama wants/to go to sleep, too."* About three to five verses of that, and I was out.

My new bedroom became a confined space, an actual lockdown at night. Each night before we went to bed, Mother would move the heavy dresser from across the room, the bed, and anything else she could find, and push it tightly against the bedroom door. Keep in mind this was the early '40s, when crime was unheard of. Mother was safe in her mind, I suppose, with all her windows secured by decorative wrought iron, and it was impossible for me to move the furniture away from her bedroom door.

I was feeling closed in; I didn't know why we were surrounded with so many obstacles. I would have opened the window and escaped after my *"Go to sleep/my Brenda Lou,"* but the wrought iron on the windows spoke to me very clearly: "You are not going anywhere." One night after we had gone to bed and Mother had gone through her ritual of securing the room, the phone rang. It was the operator telling us that she received a report that our house was on fire. Lucky for us, it was our apartment building across the street, and not our house. We would never have been able to move the bedroom furniture in time to escape the fire.

I would later learn why I was put in this confined space. My father drank a lot and became an alcoholic. He was often very drunk—and sometimes violent. On the occasions when he would come home, he would be cussing, ranting, raving, and violent. The barricaded room was where we went for protection.

When I was older, I spoke with a counselor at a spa who suggested that my childhood was like living in a dungeon. At first, I was shocked by her suggestion. But then I realized that she was exactly right. But just like the people I grew up with, I had my medicine, my love, my out, my survival mode: music.

Chapter 2

The Plantation Inn

About a year after we moved to Pine Street, in 1943, Daddy bought an old roadhouse and gambling hall at 3600 Broadway, about a mile and a half east of the dry goods store, and turned it into one of the most famous nightclubs in American history—The Plantation Inn. Daddy had lots of other businesses in West Memphis. Among other things, he opened a liquor store, a hotel and pool hall, an Arkansas souvenir shop, and two restaurants—one was a family-style restaurant, and one was in a truck stop. But the Plantation Inn, or PI, as it was known, was where he spent his time and energy.

West Memphis was famous for its nightlife—gambling, heavy drinking, risqué movies and plays, and nightclubs. Especially after midnight, Memphians who wanted to keep having fun would flock to West Memphis. "I guess West Memphis had laxer cops or something," explained Memphis musician and artist Jimmy Crosthwait. "Everybody over there was drunk; they had to get from there to here, and nobody ever seemed to stop 'em. West Memphis was where Memphians could get extra wild."

The Plantation Inn was the most popular venue of all. Unlike other nightclubs, which featured White bands playing country music, the PI had some of the best Black bands in the mid-south. It was a place where "Phineas Newborn, Sr., Ben Branch, and trumpet player Willie Mitchell led jumping little bands, where Gilbert Caple's sax and Larry Brown's bass playing continued to inspire Packy Axton and Duck Dunn, where the Largos provided near-perfect renditions of the latest hits (and steps), and where a singing waiter named Tennessee Turner, also known as 'Sissy Charles,' performed 'Danny Boy' and 'He's Got the Whole World in His Hands' at least twice nightly," says American music critic Peter Guralnik.

The Plantation Inn was hugely popular in its heyday. Everyone came: college kids, sophisticated Memphis couples, movie stars, wannabe musicians, and famous musicians, including Elvis Presley, Jerry Lee Lewis, and Charlie Rich. Alcohol could not be sold at the Plantation Inn, so my father set up a liquor store next door so people could purchase liquor and brown-bag it. We made money off the liquor sold next door and the ice buckets ordered at most of the tables. Daddy managed to have all bases covered. The admission for entering the club was $2.40 a couple.

The main room, where all the action took place, had tables on each side of the long, rectangular dance floor that stretched from the entrance to the bandstand on the far end. According to historian Robert Gordon, the spirit of the PI was "summed up on a neon sign hanging near the stage which bore the name of a radio show once hosted by the senior Berger and broadcast from the club: 'Having Fun with Morris.'" Daddy's radio show, which he broadcast live from the Plantation Inn, would start around 9:00 p.m. every evening and go until 4:00 a.m. the next day.

Lying on the top of a booth at Plantation Inn;
Daddy and Mother second and third from left

"A lot of people say the origins of the Memphis sound began at the Plantation Inn, and I think there's a lot of truth to that," said famous R&B trumpeter Wayne Jackson. "We did get ideas from those bands. We dressed up and shined our shoes and did steps." The bands at the Plantation Inn were "the single most significant influence on what became the Memphis sound," said famed Memphis music producer Jim Dickinson. "All of what became soul music was derivative of what Ben Branch and the Largos were doing. It was sort of what continued happening in the recording studios in Memphis later on—how the same group of musicians developed a kind of interplay and a style."

Red Kelly made a similar point: "The bands of Willie Mitchell, Bowlegs Miller, and Ben Branch became a proving ground for a generation of up-and-coming Memphis musicians, and provided a readily available talent pool for the explosion of small record companies and studios that grew up in the wake of Sun and Elvis." But Calvin

Newborn said it best in a 2013 interview: "There were three people who I attribute to the flourishing of Rock 'n Roll in Memphis: Sam Phillips, Morris Berger, and Elvis Presley. They were people who were way ahead of their time." So true!

One of my earliest and best memories was my mother allowing me to stay up and listen to my father's voice on the live broadcast from the PI. He would have the band play the hit song by Buddy Clark, "Linda," written by Jack Lawrence, and based on the name of his attorney Lee Eastman's daughter Linda (who would later marry Paul McCartney). But he changed the name in the lyrics to "Brenda":

> *When I go to sleep*
> *I never count sheep*
> *I count all the charms about [Brenda]*
> *And lately it seems*
> *In all of my dreams*
> *I walk with my arms about [Brenda]*

When the song ended, Daddy would always say, "Goodnight, Brenda. I love you." The words "I love you" sounded so soothing and made me happy. But I was conflicted about that personal sentiment in the song. Mother said that he did not love us, and that was why he was not home.

Pretty soon after the Plantation Inn opened, Mother sold our house on Pine Street and the cotton field behind it, and she made a lot of money from those transactions. From that point, my life became, literally, filled with music every day. We moved into the Plantation Inn, and now I was back on the wrong side of the tracks and in a bad

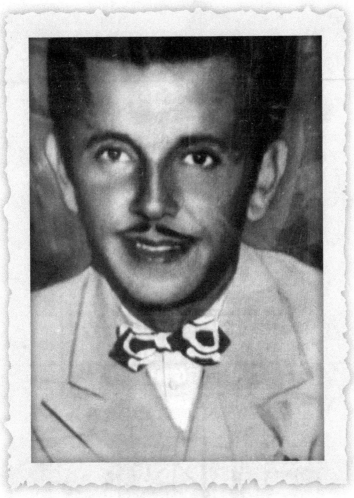

My handsome, stylish father

environment for any friends to visit. But I was surrounded by music and people I dearly loved.

The Plantation Inn nightclub was not boring at all for a little girl. I had bright lights outside my window coming from the largest neon sign in the South:

Plantation Inn sign outside my window

My room was on the second floor of the night club, and the bright lights would blink with the beat of the music downstairs. I was guided by sounds of music and the Black adults, who were all very, very kind and protective of me. Although my life was not considered normal, in the sense that my friends could not spend the day with me or sleep over, I still had the very best music in the world to listen to.

During the day I would go down to the dance floor to turn on the jukebox. The jukebox was available for customers to select a tune during the band break and continue dancing. I loved dancing the day away with Doris Day's rendition of *It's Magic* and all the other kinds of music on the jukebox: jitterbug, rhumba, waltz, and many more. The songs were a far cry from the band music in the evening. As I danced across the floor, I would make up steps as I went along.

When I tired of the dance floor, I would continue pretend-playing in other ways. I had movie magazines, from which I would cut out photos and put on my wall. I would go out on the roof of the Plantation Inn and fly a kite and watch how free it was. I planted a garden in the back of the club on our land. The dirt was perfect as it had just been tilled by the people who leased the land to grow cotton. Our nightclub was just outside the city limits, so there were no homes or businesses around—just a lot of undeveloped land. I would venture down what is now called Club Road to a sharecropper's home, sitting desolate and empty in a field nearby, behind the Plantation Inn. I walked by it every day and once went inside. It had newspaper for wallpaper, the windows were barely hanging on (the ones that were left), and the front door was missing.

Mother made sure I had an area for my garden. Watching things grow was exciting for me. I pretended that my father would finally be proud that I had radishes in the garden. They were his favorite.

But his wrath came out over dinner, when I found out I'd let them stay in the ground too long! They were way "too large," as he said in a non-appreciative tone. My father would not take one bite of a radish. He let me know I did not know what I was doing. By this time, I should have gotten the message that he bore some type of resentment that I was the one who was alive and not my sister Donna Sue.

In the evenings I would be allowed to go downstairs at 9:00 and watch the customers dance. My father would take my hand, and he and I would be in the middle of the dance floor. He was a very smooth dancer and very easy to follow. And all would say that he was more handsome than Clark Gable. When he was on the dance floor, he certainly had the attention of most of the women in the club.

Mother and Daddy dancing at the Plantation Inn

Over the years, the dances came in an array of styles: the Black Bottom, the Frug, the Waltz, the Two Step, the Shuffle, the U T Bop, the Jitterbug, the Twist, and on and on. Plus, the band would play a few Latin-American tunes and we would tango or rhumba or samba. I was so comfortable dancing with Daddy. It felt like he was showing me off—or maybe himself. I never, ever understood why he would say "Goodnight" and "I love you" over the radio show but not show his love to me when he was around me.

When I would go downstairs to the nightclub area in the evenings, I loved to observe people. I would watch a couple kiss—and the guy or the girl would be looking out at someone else. Jack Lemmon came one night and joined our table—a nice-looking young man. Other famous visitors to the Plantation Inn included Van Heflin, Dave Gardner, and Magda Gabor of the famous Gabor sisters, who rented our club for a risqué play.

If Memphis banned certain entertainment, West Memphis was available. Perhaps most famously, when Memphis placed an obscenity ban on Sam McCulloch's play *Tragic Ground*, an adaptation of an Erskine Caldwell novel, the Plantation Inn staged it to great acclaim.

Perhaps the most famous family to play at the Plantation Inn was the Newborn family—Phineas (who played drums) and his two sons Calvin (who played guitar) and Phineas, Jr. (who played piano). In addition to performing at Plantation Inn from 1947 to 1951, they played on B.B. King's first album, recorded in 1949, and followed that as session players at Sam Phillips' Sun Records.

As B.B. King once said: "My very first recordings were for a company out of Nashville called Bullet, the Bullet Record Transcription Company. I had horns that very first session. I had Phineas Newborn on piano; his father played drums, and his brother, Calvin, played guitar with me. I had Tuff Green on bass, Ben Branch on tenor sax, his brother, Thomas Branch, on trumpet, and a lady trombone player. The Newborn family were the house band at the famous Plantation Inn in West Memphis."

I would often see Elvis Presley in the club. He was there "every Wednesday and Friday nights," according to Calvin Newborn. And the main thing he did was watch the Newborn family, especially Calvin. Elvis "got rhythm from my dad, he got boogie-woogie from my brother, and he got his poise from me," Calvin once joked.

Of course, there are dozens of musicians around Memphis who'll tell you just how much Elvis got from *them*, but Calvin has a point. Back then, the youngest Newborn was a wild man, famed for a stage act that included leaping into the air in mid solo, a routine that earned him the nickname "Legs."

Prior to Calvin's death in 2018, he came to Memphis for our Plantation Inn symposium. He wrote me a letter that was enclosed with a copy of his book, *As Quiet as It's Kept! The Genius of Phineas Newborn, Jr.* and some CDs he recorded, which are priceless. The letter said:

Dear Brenda,

This is the "Phineas Newborn, Sr. Orchestra," which your Dad called "Phineas Newborn Family Band," and just a smidgen of music we played there. It was recorded in 1951 at the Flamingo Room in Memphis. Of course, we played "The Tennessee Waltz" every night for your mother and father to do their nightly eloquent dance to. They were the epitome of a successful and happy southern couple. I loved to play for them and see them dance so eloquently together. They were fabulous!

*This music reiterated how far ahead of our time and space
we were, which is probably why we were so ignored. That is,
until my brother recorded for the wealthy Texan Don Robey,
of Houston, Texas, on his "Progressive Jazz" label, then went
to the "Jazz Mountaintop," in New York with Count Basie at
Birdland, Basin Street, Carnegie Hall, etc.*

Enjoy the CDs. I love you, madly!

Calvin

Charles Turner, our gay singer with a beautiful voice, watched over
me like a hawk at the PI. When I was a teenager and came into the
club with my boyfriend Billy, he would walk up to me and say "Miss
Brenda, watch out for him"—a caution that applied to any male I
brought into the club. It did not matter who it was—he would say
the same thing. He was kind and gave me plenty of space, but I knew
that he was there and that I was safe.

Everyone thought Charles had the best voice at the Plantation
Inn. He certainly drew the crowds, and the customers loved him. His
rendition of "This Is Dedicated to the One I Love" is, to me, by far the
most beautiful song ever written—everyone would scream and holler
when he sang it. He also sang "Danny Boy," my Father's favorite, and
"Tennessee Waltz," which Mother and Daddy would often dance to.

I did not realize until much later, during a symposium on the
Plantation Inn, that the musicians made fun of Charles because he
was gay—even though they admired his talent. When my father hired
Charles, my brother Louis Jack went up to him and said: "Now you
know you are different, and you have to stay away from the customers.
Just sing with that beautiful voice, and you will be fine."

When I learned this, it made me sad. Strange how people think and say hurtful things with hate, resentment, and unkind remarks. All that should matter is the beauty and talent of the person. I will always love Charles for who he was, for his love, and for his talent. Here is a photo of him—below a banner of my father with balloons, which read: "Having Fun with Morris."

Charles Turner at the Plantation Inn

There were other ways the musicians were not always treated well. For example, I learned late in my life that they did not have a bathroom. They had an exit door behind the bandstand and had to go outside. Learning that made me unhappy.

The Plantation Inn was one of the very few places in the South where White people could come and listen to Black people play music live. There usually weren't problems, but sometimes, late in the night, after people had been drinking, and when some of the White ladies would pay too much attention to Black band members, or when the Black band members would leave the bandstand and enter the dancing area, things would get touchy. "Fights almost happened a few times, but Mr. Morris controlled it," recalled Calvin Newborn. "He'd go get him a drink of that Hill & Hill, and he'd straighten it out. He was a good man, but he loved that Hill and Hill. And I loved Mr. Morris."

So many of the bands and performers who got their start at the Plantation Inn went on to be famous or influential in American music.

Me and Floyd Newman in 2013

Floyd Newman was a jazz saxophonist in the regular band that played at the Plantation Inn. One night, Daddy fired the leader (I cannot remember his name) and asked Floyd to take charge. Floyd eventually put together a band that included Isaac Hayes on keyboards, Howard Grimes on drums, and Joe Woods on guitar. This was the beginning of Floyd's career as a bandleader, and the first big break for Isaac Hayes, who would, of course, have a great career, including winning an Academy Award for the theme song in *Shaft*. Tim Sampson, the communications director for the Soulsville Foundation, said that, during Floyd's time at the Plantation Inn, he became "very instrumental in helping create what is known as the 'Memphis Sound.'" I love you, Floyd; you had such talent.

Me and Isaac Hayes in 2013

When The Newborns left us in 1951, they toured with Jackie Brenston and played on the record *Rocket 88*, which some people consider to be the first Rock 'n Roll record. Phineas Jr. went on to be a famous jazz pianist, and Calvin toured in the 1960s with many famous musicians, including Lionel Hampton, Wild Bill Davis, Freddie Roach, and Booker Little, and he worked with Ray Charles and Count Basie, among others.

Willie Mitchell, the trumpeter, went on to become a famous recording artist and producer. Bowlegs Miller, another trumpeter, became a famous performer on Beale Street and produced many famous singers, including Al Green, Otis Redding, Aretha Franklin, and Lou Rawls. Ben Branch became a famous jazz saxophonist and bandleader; he was also one of the last people Martin Luther King spoke with before he died. There are many other examples.

Chapter 3

The Birth of Pancho's

The Plantation Inn was not Daddy's only business. He had many others, in addition to the dry goods store. He built a hotel on Broadway between 13th and 14th street. It was narrow but went back very deep and had a pool hall on the bottom floor. I was seven or eight years old when he built it, and it was fun to watch it go up.

I once tried to climb the stairs that went to the top floor in the middle of construction. My father allowed me to climb it because, he said, "What goes up has to come down." Each step had a huge gap; one misstep and you would definitely go down quick. It was a challenge, but it was fun. And it taught me a lesson that stuck with me: If I do wrong, I can undo the wrong; if I go in the wrong direction, I can change directions; if I make a mess, I can clean it up; if I wrote a song I did not like, I could change the lyrics; and so on. This idea seemed to apply to my whole life.

Daddy also owned a laundromat on Broadway. And he had several businesses on two properties at the triangle corner where Interstate 55 and Route 70 met on the east end of town. These busy roads were split like a piece of pie—Route 70 continued west through the middle of West Memphis, and Interstate 55 went west and then north, all the way to St. Louis and beyond. On those spots he placed five trolley cars that he had Mother buy in St. Louis.

Two of the cars were diners. One diner car was the entrance. It had a bar, open kitchen, and seating area with two pinball machines. The state of Arkansas eventually confiscated (and then destroyed) the pinball machines; they were deemed "gambling devices," since we paid off high-score winners. The second, connected dining car was where people ate. A third trolley car, connected to the restaurant, sold souvenirs.

Across Route 70 on Interstate 55, Daddy had property where he built a liquor store and another restaurant in the other two trolley cars. These were great locations, and all the hungry truckers would stop by for the Bergers' fast food. As a teenager, I would sometimes fill in as a cook. I once lost a false fingernail. I have no idea which trucker had the delicious nail in his food.

We also had firecracker stands on many properties. I worked in one of them around the New Year holiday, freezing to death with a heater inside the stand with thousands of dollars' worth of fireworks. I also worked as an underage girl selling liquor in our liquor business. And when I was not selling liquor, I was doing the books in the back office.

On the weekends, I would sometimes be asked to accompany one of the bands at the Plantation Inn to a college. I once as a teenager went to the University of Arkansas to a fraternity dance with the Vel Tones, whom the college students loved. My mother's friend Mrs. Johnson accompanied me. Good thing, because coming home I was falling asleep at the wheel around 2:00 a.m. But we made it home safely.

After about a decade running the Plantation Inn, after it became a famous institution, Daddy stopped his radio show and let my brother Louis Jack run the PI. Louis Jack changed things a bit, adding tea dances on Sunday afternoons. It was about that time, in the summer of 1955, that Daddy made his biggest move. He took Louis Jack on a graduation trip to Guaymas, Mexico. They stayed at the Hotel Playa de Cortes and did a lot of fishing.

Daddy and Louis Jack in Guaymas, Mexico

They also ate at lots of restaurants. Daddy talked to the cooks at the ones he liked best, and he came back home with lots of recipe ideas that he experimented with and tested. Thus was born the idea for Pancho's Mexican Restaurants. Daddy perfected many recipes, most famously, Pancho's cheese dip, which is now sold in retail stores (including Kroger and Walmart) in many states.

Daddy first opened Pancho's on our property behind the trolley cars on Route 70. There was a deserted building that had a tree growing—inside—in the back. Daddy fixed it up and decorated it with cowhide booths and tables with romantic lighting—he called it "Lovers' Lane." We put a Lovers' Lane into many of the restaurants. It was especially popular in West Memphis as a meeting place for couples from Memphis.

The first Pancho's, with a tree inside

One afternoon, at one of the trolley cars, Daddy was drawing what would become the Pancho's Man—the logo for the restaurant. After he completed the drawing, he asked me what I thought. I pointed out a few things that I thought would add to the character of the Pancho's man.

Oh, boy—my mistake. Daddy got furious with me and treated me badly for nothing. I broke down finally and ran out of the trolley car and hid in the old dirt-floor building that Daddy was going to renovate for Pancho's. I found a corner, sat down, and cried my heart out. I am sure the only company I had were rats, because the building had been isolated for years out in a field. Finally, Mother showed up and took me home.

In 1965, a truck ran through Pancho's and destroyed it. We decided to build a new bigger and better Pancho's on the same property as the Plantation Inn. And soon after we built the new Pancho's, we closed and demolished the PI and built a parking lot that would serve the new building on the adjacent property. The entrance had a covered wagon that we later put on the roof for many years. The restaurant had many rooms and was very quaint. In the front, there were two rooms. Then came a bar area, with bar stools along the bar and four booths behind. Further back was the huge banquet room that had private booth areas on each side.

At that time, all of the food was cooked on the premises. The cheese dip is famous, but also great were the salsa, Pancho's dressing (which went on tacos, nachos, and more), laredos, and what I thought was the very best chili in the world. (We also served Daddy's amazing tamales, which were so good that he opened up a tamale shop in Memphis called *Jack's Tamales*). For a while, Pancho's was open 24 hours a day and served breakfast. I sometimes worked the graveyard shift, from midnight until 8 a.m., and cooked.

We also built a Go-Go lounge in the rear of Pancho's called the "El Toro Lounge." The girls were instructed to wear very short mini-skirts and tight or strapless tops. The dance floor was very small, unlike the huge one at the Plantation Inn. There was a very long bar the length of the lounge. Liquor was sold in the lounge, which was a change after all the years that the Plantation Inn had been dry.

The new Pancho's, before the Plantation Inn was demolished

I helped in the founding of Pancho's in various ways. Louis Jack and I walked the property and laid out the restaurant and lounge. We hired Mexican workers to do the front of the restaurant. We wanted an authentic look, and they deliberately built the building with crooked bricks, to look old. I created the first menus as well. My brother Louis Jack asked me to paint the menus on pieces of wood—100 menus in all—shaped like a paddle. (Later we switched to coated paper menus).

At some point, we opened a restaurant on Bellevue Avenue in Memphis. It was located near Graceland, and Elvis would sometimes stop in to eat. (He was also buried, at first, in the cemetery across from the restaurant, but his body was later moved to Graceland.) The Bellevue restaurant had a "tree" in the main dining room made of real tree bark and silk green leaves—it was a nice effect. The kitchen was located to make sure the plates came out quickly and hot. I sometimes worked the night shift in this restaurant.

We closed at 11:00 p.m. I would then drive home, using the narrow road through the cemetery that led to Park Avenue and eventually to the bridge to Arkansas. One night I caught a light on Park. A man came up to my passenger door and tried to get into my car. Luckily, the door was locked. I gunned the car and took off, hoping that I was not dragging the man connected to my door. I had all of the money from the evening to deposit at the bank the next day on the seat near me!

Chapter 4

Bertha

Bertha Smith was a Black woman who started to take care of me when she was 13 years old and I was three years old. Bertha and I would be close all of our lives.

Bertha's mother, Bessie, started working for Mother when we first bought the little house on Pine Street. Bessie had met Mother at our dry goods store. Bessie and her family came from Chatfield, Arkansas. Chatfield was only 10 miles from where my father and I would go fishing: Horseshoe Lake.

Bertha told me many great stories about her life before she moved from Chatfield to West Memphis. The owner of the cotton field where Bessie's husband worked saw her taking him food out in the fields for lunch. The owner scolded Bessie and said he was not going to allow him to work in the fields. Bessie said, "Fine, but I'm takin' my husband some food."

Then the owner went to Bessie's husband and told him what Bessie had said. He told the owner, "Well, if that is what Bessie said, that is what Bessie means—fine!" So, the owner paid them their daily pay and fired them, which is what led Bessie's family to move to West Memphis, and that's how Bertha came into my life.

Bertha and Bessie, but mainly Bertha, were by my side until I left home to get married and beyond. Bertha would tell me stories of Mother being pregnant with me. She said Clemmye was so beautiful and would walk the other side of Broadway North on Eighth Street every day from the store. Mother would later say that, before she walked, she would eat an apple. Food was scarce, and apples were very filling for Mother. I am surprised I was not born with an apple in my mouth, because Mother would always tell me the story of how many apples she ate carrying me.

My life as a young child appeared to be normal. I would sometimes make mud pies on the side of the Pine Street house, ride my stationary leather pony, or play with my dolls and my piano. I looked like a little Indian girl, with long black hair and dark skin. In the daytime I would play outside with friends when I wasn't with Mother. At night we would catch the lightning bugs in a glass jar and play hide-and-seek. At an early age, there was a boy I liked. At a birthday party, I rigged the drawings so that the boy I liked could win a prize. Shame on me, but it made him happy.

Often, when I was playing, I would watch how hard the men, women, and children worked in the cotton fields behind our house, and I wanted to do something. Almost every day, I had Bertha make a huge jar of lemonade. Bertha and I would take the lemonade out to the cotton fields behind our home to give it to the men, women, and children picking cotton.

Lemonade was my small way of helping. The cotton-field workers allowed me to work/play in the fields and pick cotton. It was fun, but I only pulled out the cotton from the bolls and gave it to someone. I did not have to carry the heavy knapsack. I did not have the long days and constant bending of the body, prickling of the fingers, and Lord knows what else they endured.

Bertha once said, "Miss Brenda, I am scared to death of those worms!" She was referring to boll weevils, an ugly insect that feeds on cotton buds and flowers. Bertha told me that, when she lived with her family in Chatfield as sharecroppers, she worked in the cotton fields. "I never complained except for one thing, and that was those green and white worms on those cotton bolls," she told me. "Don't know why, but I was scared to death of them. I would run home and tell Mom, but she would give me a whoopin' and tell me to get back into the fields."

Bertha would use her daily pay to buy thick bologna slices and crackers, and large drinks, like Nehi—the larger the better. She did not drink Coca-Cola, though, since Black people were not allowed to buy it. But Bertha did not mind that she could not buy Coke, because the Nehi grape drinks were bigger.

Mother would often have Bertha and me go to Memphis to shop for her. (Mother knew how to spend money for her own pleasure, which I admired, since she also gave money to anyone in need). Bertha and I would wait for the bus. We entered the bus, and she went to the back of the bus, where she had to go. I followed along and sat in the back as well, as I did not want to be in the front without Bertha.

We got into Memphis and would go into Levy's on the corner of Union and Main, the top store on Main St. The other stores that Mother liked were Julius Lewis, where my Aunt Opal worked as a saleslady for many years. Other stores were Gerbers and Goldsmiths. It was strange how many Jewish families were merchants, including my father.

The packages mother had ordered were waiting for us at Levy's on the second floor. Poor Bertha was panicked and anxious about riding the elevator, which scared her. I told her that she had to, in order to collect Mother's clothes. Bertha almost had a heart attack but survived, and we collected the packages.

Our instructions from Mother were to bring the boxes she had ordered back and put them under the front door steps if my father's car was there; she was worried that Daddy would get mad. Mother would eventually try on the clothes, and, then, if she did not like them, Bertha and I had to go return the clothes. Again, the same routine, bus, back of the bus, elevator, and Bertha would almost have another heart attack.

When I was older, Bertha could drive us places, and we had a lot of fun. Going to Memphis was better, since we did not have to deal with the bus issues. We were free to do as we pleased, but Bertha was very protective and made sure we were both safe. We would walk up and down Main Street in Memphis before doing our chores for my Mother. One day we passed the Planters Peanut mascot. I told Bertha that my brother was afraid of the mascot. Bertha said he did not understand where the peanut came from, and that made sense.

While Bertha and I found a way around segregated transportation on our Memphis trips because she could drive, we could not do this for longer trips. For example, I wanted to visit my cousins—JW's daughters—in Yazoo City, Mississippi, by train. If Bertha had come with me, she would have had to ride in the second-rate "Jim Crow car" made out of wood and right behind the toxic coal coming out of the locomotive. It was very dangerous, and, if there was a train wreck the Jim Crow car would be crushed (this often happened).

Since Bertha could not accompany me, Mother's friend Arcadia Johnson did. She was a nice lady who had a large indentation in her head from a car accident. Mrs. Johnson and I arrived at Yazoo City, and I was so excited. My uncle had a storefront with refrigerators in

Bertha with my son Jack, in 1963

the window, and they lived above the store. He had many patents for parts for the refrigerator that made him a millionaire. My oldest cousin, Donna Kay, seemed so grown up and sophisticated. I felt a bit out of place with her. Jerry Ann was more my age, and we played quite a bit. I stayed for only two days but enjoyed my first outing from

West Memphis. Yazoo City was quite a pretty town and was named after the Indian tribe that lived on the river's mouth.

Once Bessie was working at the Plantation Inn, cleaning the part of the building that was our home, and she left the living-room door open to air out the room. Suddenly she was confronted by a drifter who was hungry, dirty, and very scary looking. Bessie screamed; her scream echoed through the building as Bertha and I returned home. We ran to find Bessie hiding under a table and booth in the back of the nightclub. She told us why she was screaming and hiding.

We turned around to see if the man was still in the building. But he had started walking down Highway 70. He seemed to me to be drunk or out of it because he was swaying from side to side. We could not get Bessie out from under the table until my mother came home and said, "Bessie, Brenda and I will take you home, where you will feel safe." Mother was always saving people; she would grab me in the process, as if I were a rag doll.

One day we got an urgent call from Bessie: "Mrs. Clemmye, please come quick! Ernest is killing Bertha." Ernest was Bertha's husband. He traveled on the road with B.B. King, taking care of his instruments. He got to know King, since just down the road from Bertha's house on Sixteenth Street was the Square Deal Café—also known as Miss Annie's café—where B.B. King performed and lived.

Bertha and Ernest had not been married very long. They had been fighting, and Ernest had thrown Bertha in the ditch in front of their house on Sixteenth Street. Mother and I jumped into her convertible. As we drove up with the top down, Bertha and her husband were rolling in the muddy ditch. Poor Bertha was being drowned in the mud.

Clemmye parked the car, got out, and walked up to Ernest. She was only five feet tall, and he was huge. She looked up at the muscular man and told him—in no uncertain terms—never to lay another hand on Bertha. Ernest listened and never hurt Bertha again. I will never forget Bertha's eyes. They were swollen almost shut from the beating, and her face was just a black ball of mud. Anyway, Mother saved the day.

Chapter 5

My Amazing Mother

My mother, Clemmye, was a kind lady with a giving spirit that poured from her very quietly to help people in need. I spent a lot of time in my youth with Bertha, but I spent more time with my mother. She was my guiding light, someone I adored and truly looked up to. For the first eighteen years of my life, I was by her side as if I were an appendage of her body. We slept in the same room, and we drove everywhere together. We traveled together and we rescued people together. She and I read the horoscope together, side by side, every morning. We were on the same wavelength—both Virgos.

When I was old enough, the routine was to help mother, mainly with her business errands. After getting up in the morning, eating, and getting dressed, we would open the safe, count the money, make out the deposit slips, and go to the bank, where we would deposit the money, and where mother would sometimes borrow money for Daddy's new ventures. All the bankers respected Mother. When she borrowed, she paid on time and paid the loan off.

When I was a teenager, about 15, while Mother was wheeling and dealing at the bank in Memphis, I decided to do a little wheeling and dealing of my own. I found a banker with an empty desk and introduced myself. I told her I worked for Clemmye Berger and what I earned weekly. Then I told her that I would like to get a loan to buy my mother a fur coat for her birthday.

I did get the loan and, walking in my mother's footsteps, I paid it off on time. Mother was expressionless when I gave her the coat for

My mother, Clemmye Berger

her birthday, and, of course, I was a bit disappointed. I don't know and never did know what was going on in her mind. Maybe she thought I stole the coat.

Taking the cash to the bank was just one way Mother controlled the money going in and out of the businesses. She also made sure all the property and businesses were in her name. Daddy had the ideas, but Mother was the businessperson, the rational, organized one. She was just as important to our family's success as Daddy. Together, they made excellent business partners.

Don't ask me why Mother would put her signature and businesses on the line for Daddy to keep buying, building, and drinking. I will never know the answer to that. But he was a genius with business ideas and very creative artistically. Bertha would say, simply, "Your mother loves him." Mother supported him throughout her life, even when he was with other women, and even after they divorced. This seemed odd to me; I never got used to it.

Our next stop was to go to our dry goods store and other businesses. I would stay all day and pretend I was selling clothes. I actually started trying shoes on customers and thinking that, in some small way, I was helping. Mother allowed me to decorate the window and put the dresses, shoes, belts, overalls, and whatever I could find to make it look pretty. On weekends, the store was open until 9:00 p.m.

Our dry goods store, like others, would select a specific line of merchandise to accommodate the customer. There were lots of textiles, thread, needles, shoes for specific requests, bows, ribbon, blue jeans, Big Johns, shirts, robes, gowns, and more. When a customer made a request, we brought the items into our store. Mother would take her list to Memphis, and we would go shopping at Becks for hats and

William R. Moore for all of the textiles and fill-ins for just about everything requested. Our customers loved this special attention.

There was a package chute at the store that fascinated me. As we would get off on each floor, the chute was open all the way down on each floor. I would be looking around, and, all of a sudden, I would hear a "swoosh," and down came a huge package on its way to the bottom floor of the building. The warehouse was about six stories tall. When we would get to the first floor, I would see all of the packages piled up ready for delivery.

Driving with Mother was a wild experience. She took to the middle of the road and dared anyone to pass her. She claimed it was her highway and she would not budge. We were once on our way to Huntsville, Alabama, to visit my brother in the service. Again the top was down, and I felt the wind hard against my face, as if we were flying instead of driving. Mother had her pedal to the metal. I looked at the speedometer, and, sure enough, we were going 120 miles an hour. When I told Mother she was cruising at 120 miles an hour and warned her that she would get a speeding ticket, she just laughed and stayed at the same speed, daring any cop to catch up with her. Life with Mother was like living on the edge.

Many Sundays were family days. Mother, Daddy, I, and sometimes my brother Louis Jack, would drive to Memphis over the old Harahan Bridge. It was one lane going, and, on the other side, it was one lane coming back. In between the span of the two roads were two railroad tracks used by the Missouri Pacific and Rock Island Railroads, to name a few.

When there was a wreck or breakdown, everyone would, of course, have to wait, and my curious nature would draw me to open the door behind Daddy and see what was happening. My ten pounds at birth had developed into a chubby little girl, but I was still able to fall through the guard railings on the bridge. Fortunately, Mother was quick and pulled me back. There was a gap at the bottom of the railings that I could easily have fallen through. This was my third close call with death. I stayed around to live a very colorful life.

My father was sometimes very violent when he was drunk. He would mostly get drunk at night, but, as the years went on, he had no time clock. On one of our Sunday trips to Memphis, he drank a lot. On the way home from Memphis, he ranted and raved, and called Mother names that were new to me. The "F" word was flying across the center of my head through my ears to Mother's ears.

I should have realized from my vantage point in the middle of the front seat that I would be stuck in the middle of a crisis for many years to come. I wanted to run away. Throughout the years I had a desperate yearning to run, to be alone. Thank God I grew up around music. It lifted me up as always.

Because of his all-night music show, and because he was often drunk, and who knows for what other reasons, Daddy was not home very much when we lived on Pine Street. When Daddy did come home, he was, as I noted above, often violent, and would slam his fist through the wall. Daddy's visits were marked by the new photos on the wall needed to cover the holes he made.

Sometimes he was so violent that Mother would grab me when the moment was right, and we would bolt out of the back door and go hide in the cotton fields behind the house. I was not in the bedroom-dungeon; I was now confined in a row in the cotton fields. Just another unusual place to sleep.

As time passed, Mother would track Daddy's movements when he would leave one of our businesses. She knew if he was sober or drinking through her sources. If he was sober, all was all right for us to see him, but the more he drank, the more new places I had to spend the night in another type of bed. Mother and I stuck together like glue and were always on the run. We would hide at our hotel and have the room checked off as occupied. Those beds were spring-type cots.

Mother would often have Mrs. Johnson or someone else drop us off at our hiding place so that our car would not be around. Then there was the laundromat that Mrs. Johnson owned. We would hide out there but then go home with her when she closed her business for the day. We would spend the night with her, two bedrooms and, again, twin beds in each. The irony of this was that we were hiding from an alcoholic and spending the night at the home of another alcoholic—Mrs. Johnson's husband—but he was usually sleeping.

Unfortunately, the safe house at Mrs. Johnson's house became a nightmare for me. When I was about seven, Mother would have me dropped off at Mrs. Johnson's home after school sometimes and come to pick me up several hours later. I was there alone with Mr. Johnson. As time went by, Mr. Johnson wanted me to lie down in bed with him to rest, and he would begin stroking and feeling my whole body. That was my first experience of child abuse, and I kept it within myself. I would squirm and then say I was hungry and jump out of bed and go to the kitchen.

Once I was out of bed, he allowed me my freedom. I stayed in the kitchen until Mother arrived. I had no one to tell, or at least I did not have anyone I felt loved me enough to understand. I did tell my mother once when I was angry, probably when I was in my 40s. Her reaction was nothing: no words, absolutely nothing, almost a state of denial. The lesson I learned: you cannot really trust men you *think* you can trust with your child.

I took many wild trips with Mother, in and out of town. One winter day when I was young, and Daddy was messing around with other women, Mother decided that she and I would play detective. We hopped in her El Dorado Cadillac—her "rescue mobile"—to make sure Daddy wasn't misbehaving. (In my experience then and later, males were always misbehaving and not trustworthy).

We drove to a modest home, in a nice neighborhood, and approached the front door, which Mother opened. (I'm not sure how she knew where to go). There were four couples, a prominent doctor and lawyer, a veterinarian that I knew, and Daddy, all with their mistresses. I stayed by the door and watched Mother take over, and all hell broke loose. She picked up a fur coat that belonged to one of the ladies and started tearing it into shreds. "Morris, you are no good!" my mother screamed. She grabbed me again, and out the door we went.

Mother's remark that Daddy was rarely home because he did not love us has remained embedded in my mind until this day. I remember very few days with him at home. He never took time with me at home, but I would get the privilege of rubbing his back and feet when he did make it home. One holiday, he was home, and we were having a nice dinner. Then out of nowhere, he got mad at me. I was not as afraid of Daddy as Mother was. He made me leave the table and go to the bathroom. He shut the door but did not lock it.

I do not remember what caused the disagreement, but I ended up getting a belt-whipping because I would not give in to his demands. This shows you how stubborn I was, because I knew I had not done anything wrong. He could have killed me, and I would have stood my ground. My mother, brother, and my father's mother, "Big Mama," did not open their mouths during the abuse. He finally stopped after screaming at me very loudly and hitting me several times.

I did see Daddy along with Mother sometimes at the construction site of the hotel, or I would watch him play pool with some guys. When no one was around in the pool hall, I would grab a stick and take a few shots at the balls. I was very adventurous, probably also bored and feeling alone. Possibly wanting to be noticed.

When I was twelve years old, Mother did something that ignited my temper. I was coming up the stairs in our home part of the Plantation Inn, and when I rounded the corner, my mother was in the hallway, kissing a man. I threw a fit, ran into her bedroom, slammed the door, and started tearing her bedspread to pieces. I later learned that this man was President of Bethlehem Steel. She did let me know that I'd messed up what could have been a good thing for her. If it weren't for my tantrum, Mother would own lots of stock in Bethlehem Steel.

I, of course, did not feel guilty at all. Mother did not punish me or mention anything about the bedspread. *Why* I don't know. She never raised her voice to me. Do you think I was spoiled? Maybe she wanted me to have a mind of my own, which I certainly did. My mother was so gentle with me. She was a giving soul.

Mother was mean to me only once, years later, after the birth of my third child, Steven. I was in the Crittenden hospital after having a partial hysterectomy. If I moved in the slightest way, I would be in excruciating pain. I asked Mother to use the controls to raise my head, but to do it very, very slowly. She turned a crank hard, and I went up very quickly. Another crank in the opposite direction, and I went down very quickly. This continued until I was in a cold sweat and nearly faint. She found this very amusing and continued laughing while she tortured her daughter.

Mother was always taking care of Daddy and letting him do his thing, but he knew what his limitations were. She bought Daddy a

Winnebago to tour in. Before taking off for Florida, for some reason, he opened another nightclub and called it the Hi Hat Club. Daddy had a room in the back of the club, and I would go visit once in a while.

One day I walked in, and Daddy was in bed with a woman, and my brother was there also. I still loved my father, but things were not affecting me anymore. What else could I experience or see? Eventually Daddy tired of the nightclub business and was ready to take off in his new Winnebago. My grandmother, "Big Mama," took in the money for my father at the nightclub. Thank goodness for mothers—always there for their children. Little did I know the experiences lying ahead of me would be even more dramatic.

Chapter 6

School Days

When I was a little girl, I took a school bus to Hulbert School just outside the city limits of West Memphis. I became the drum majorette for the band, and, of course, I enjoyed it because of the music.

I attended only the first grade there, and then my mother transferred me to Miss Lee's School of Childhood in Memphis for kindergarten through sixth grade. My brother was in charge of taking me to school and picking me up for the second grade. I loved Miss Lee's school. Miss Lee lived with her younger sister, Miss Atkins, at the school. They were direct descendants of Robert E. Lee. Miss Lee was deaf and wore hearing aids that would whistle, and she would constantly be adjusting them.

Miss Lee tried to teach me several important things. One was to chew your food at least 100 times before swallowing. Of course, this is one wise thing that I omitted from my life. I never tried it even once. I learned to dance and would stay after school for piano lessons and wait for my brother to pick me up. We put on a great dance recital and were all butterflies, with long sticks to make our wings. The sheer material wrapped around the sticks made the effect beautiful.

Brenda Berger

In May, we had the May Day dance, held outside around the playground. I was selected to be on the May Day court and have a photo sitting on top of the stage with me in the middle and two friends on either side. I respected Miss Lee, loved the different activities, and especially loved to play hopscotch and climb on the monkey bars before school. Then I would be ready for my small class—three girls and four boys. We were all very close.

The next year, when it was time for third grade, I did not return to Miss Lee's. My brother dropped me off at a Catholic school instead. No one told me I would be attending a new school. and I was in a daze since I did not know what was going on. A nun was my teacher. I did not know a single person in the class, and I didn't like it. At the end of the day, the nun said, "Tomorrow, September 8, is the birthday of someone we all love," and asked us to come dressed nicely for a party to celebrate.

Miss Lee's School of Childhood

When I came home that night, I was ecstatic. I told my mother I had to go to school the next day dressed up for a birthday party the school was giving me. I arrived at school in my finest attire and sat at my desk, wiggly and excited. The nun came in and asked us to rise for catechism. I had no idea what that was. I still don't know. I moved my lips as if I understood, made it to the end, and sat down.

As I was adjusting my skirt and getting more and more excited for my birthday party, the nun motioned for silence. I expected to hear my name. "Today," she said, "we celebrate the birthday of the Virgin Mary." I was disappointed and angry. When I got home after school, I exploded. "I will not go back to that school!" I told my mother. "I will never go to school unless it is Miss Lee's."

I later learned that it was my brother's idea for me to attend the Catholic school. He was attending Christian Brothers High School in Memphis. That school was all boys, but my school had girls and boys. My brother, who was eight years older than me, wanted to meet the girls at the Catholic school. Miss Lee's school went only from kindergarten to sixth grade. The Catholic school I was attending went to twelfth grade, which was perfect for my brother, who was interested in the beautiful eleventh- and twelfth-grade Southern belles.

My temper fit won the day. I was dropped off at Miss Lee's the next day after Mother contacted Miss Lee's school. This was one of many difficulties I had with my brother Louis Jack. The eight years difference between us meant we didn't have much in common. In some ways, I idolized him. I thought he was so handsome; he was popular with the girls and was a good dancer. But often, he neglected me or was demeaning. I became jealous of the girls he was treating so nicely, since I rarely got his attention.

Sometimes, I would see my brother out in our yard playing ball and wished I could play. He would go to the movies with a bunch of his friends, and again, I wished I could go. At times, I would ask

My brother Louis Jack

Mother why I couldn't join Louis Jack. After a while, she would allow me, but I was a young child, and my brother was eleven.

The movie theater was on Broadway and Missouri. I think it was a Gene Autry western—*Back in the Saddle*. It cost 25 cents to get into the movies. The popcorn was 10 cents. I never got candy. But

I loved the original bubble gum. I was considered a tag-along and would have to sit by myself in the movie house. Even from a distance, I knew I was really just in his way. I was good and waited in my seat until Louis Jack came by to pick me up.

In one of my last years at Miss Lee's, I was selected as Cotton Carnival Princess at about age eight or nine. It was the first of many pageants I would participate in. In seventh grade, I went back to Hulbert school in Hulbert, a town southwest of West Memphis. And from grades eight to twelve, I went to West Memphis High School. During most of this period, I was in love with William Cooper Smith, better known as Billy Smith.

Billy lived around the corner from the apartment we moved to, across the street from our old home on Pine Street. When I was in about seventh grade, I first noticed him walking by our apartment a couple of times a week. I loved everything about him—especially his good looks, but also the way he walked and dressed. At this point he was just a dream, but I hoped that someday we would get together.

When I went to high school, I was grown-up in my mind. I went out for cheerleading and made the team. I had good friends and was voted the most popular girl and most beautiful. I would still dream of Billy. When I passed him in the halls, I was so excited. I would go to his football and basketball games and watch him play. At one point I was voted Queen of the Lower School football team and was hoping that he would be at the lower-school football games.

Finally, when I was in the tenth grade and Billy was in twelfth, Billy stopped dating the girl he had been dating and asked me out. I was in heaven. He was good-looking, loved the outdoors, and was very athletic; we had a lot in common—except for dancing. His father was a farmer; Billy would pick me up in his jeep, and we would go to the levee and ride horses or go see the farm and feed the pigs and chickens. I hurt my leg riding horses because my jeans were rolled up to my knees. I managed to get a bad saddle burn on my calf.

When I sold fireworks, Billy would arrive late at night to take me home. He would wait in his car to stay warm. In the middle of December, selling fireworks was miserable. I had a heater at my feet, which could have blown me to bits if I wasn't cautious. My guardian angel was still with me. I am a huge believer in guardian angels, and I know my sister Donna is mine. I hope that, when I walk through heaven's gates, she is one of the first to greet me. I would love to know her.

Billy and I were together constantly, and I was very much in love. Some days, if I had time, I would ride with him on his job to survey the land around the county. When I had my first kiss with Billy, my dream really came true. He asked me to go steady with him, and heaven had arrived. As time went on, we made out. But we didn't sleep together; I remained a virgin. At this point, the happiest part of my life was being with Billy.

Billy went to college, the University of Mississippi, on a baseball scholarship, when I started eleventh grade. I would often drive to Oxford, Mississippi, about an hour and a half south of Memphis, to see him. Sometimes we would watch Ole Miss football games, and other times, we would just hang out. I would never stay overnight; I would always drive home at the end of the day. Billy and I continued to date for my last two years in high school. We had so much fun.

My relationship with Billy marked the point at which my relationship with Mother began to change, for two reasons. First, Mother sometimes seemed jealous of my life and even my looks. When I became interested in boys, starting with Billy, she would always try to break up the relationship. In my heart, I think she did this because she lost her first daughter, Donna Sue, and did not want to lose me to others. Loss is loss; my dating and becoming serious with men was a threat to her.

Second, after Mother and Daddy divorced in the late 1950s, she developed a life of her own. She began to travel with friends and other men, and to enjoy herself, even as she continued throughout my life to intervene in my relationships.

When Mother realized things were getting serious between me and Billy, she started driving a wedge between us. She would tell me he was not good enough for me, that he was a country boy, that I could do better and be happier with someone else. This was

Me and Billy

the downside to my mother being so wonderful to me: she tried to control my life, sometimes too much. When she said these things about Billy, I got upset inside but didn't say anything to her. I have to admit that Mother's disapproval of Billy affected me and our relationship.

During my teenage years, both during and after high school, I participated in a number of beauty contests. I was Miss Junior West Memphis in 1956 or 1957, Miss Jaycee in 1957, and Miss West Memphis and Miss Congeniality in 1958. As Miss West Memphis, I competed in the Miss Arkansas contest, a step before the Miss America contest. I was also Miss Teenage Arkansas and participated in the first national Miss Teenage America contest.

Other beauty pageants I participated in included the 1960 Miss Poultry contest, the 1957 Cotton picking beauty contest, and, in the fall of my freshman college year, the Orange Bowl queen contest. I don't know why I participated in so many beauty contests. Ann Payton, a friend of Mother's, encouraged me to enter them, and one thing led to another.

In high school, I was also voted most popular and most beautiful many times. I won many honors, including most popular, most beautiful, lower-school homecoming queen, Cotton Boll maid, National Beta Club, first Vice-president of the Future Homemakers of America, and many more.

I was also a cheerleader every year in high school. To make the team, I did a cheer in the gym in front of the whole school. The cheer was "Beef Steak," and the first lines were, "Can you give it, can you take it, can you Alabama shake it." Don't ask me why "Alabama shake it" was part of the cheer. The most fun was when I was cheering on the sidelines during football games.

Me as Miss West Memphis

One day during my senior year in high school, 1957, my father brought the first hardtop convertible car—a 1957 red-and-white Ford Skyliner—to my school to surprise me. I was at softball practice, and he just left the car there at school with the keys in it. I was so excited!

And I was surprised. The first time I learned to drive on the dirt roads by our nightclub, I asked Daddy if I could show him how good I was at driving. He agreed.

Cheerleading Squad, second from right

Things went OK until I turned the corner to come back to the club. When we reached the front of the club to park the car, I put my foot on the accelerator instead of the brakes. Fortunately, I found and hit the brakes just before plowing into his prize possession: the huge Plantation Inn sign, the largest neon sign in the South. Daddy exited the car quickly, saying, "I will never, ever, ever drive with you again."

Famous last words. It is strange how time takes care of things. I am a big believer in that. When Daddy got older and needed me, I drove him to doctors, hospitals, to get groceries, and more. Also, my father mellowed quite a bit as he got older, and we became close and kind of buddies. He loved to fish and taught me how to fish when I was a young girl, which I will love forever. To this day, when I get on a lake to fish, I think of my father in a great way.

During high school, I continued to meet interesting people who would come to the Plantation Inn. One night the famous bandleader Jimmy Dorsey came to the PI after finishing a show in Memphis. Daddy placed him at the first table by the entrance, which was where he would usually seat special guests. Dorsey had a good time and invited us to dinner the next evening at the Peabody Hotel in Memphis. I enjoyed listening to him talk about music.

At Dinner with Jimmy Dorsey and my family

During my senior year, my brother got married after attending the University of Arkansas for one year. He married a woman he'd met at the Plantation Inn, Bettye Jo Elliot. Bettye was a disc jockey on Sam Phillips' all-girl Memphis radio station and had been previously married. They moved into our apartment building in West Memphis for their first home. Bettye soon got pregnant and had an adorable baby boy, Morris Jack Berger.

I did some babysitting when he was a newborn. Louis Jack decided the Planation Inn was getting dated and should be torn down to make room for the new Pancho's building and a new nightclub with a disco theme, The El Toro Lounge. We also needed a larger parking lot for customers. The newer Pancho's came about because the first one, after about six months of being open, was hit by a semitrailer. Prior to its being devastated, Governor Faubus stopped in as our first celebrity. He was known for defying a Federal Court order to integrate a school in Little Rock, Arkansas.

When I graduated from high school, class of 1958, Mother was the only one who showed up. That was okay, because I had at least one member of my family to see me graduate. One of my favorite songs they played was "You'll Never Walk Alone." Another was "I Believe." My high school graduation took me back to my kindergarten graduation. Big Mama was the only one who'd attended, and she managed to put my hat on wrong, she did not know how the graduation hats and tassels were supposed to go on. One thing for sure, I stood out in our graduation group photo.

For my graduation, my mother wrote me a "penance" on a piece of grocery bag. Here is what it said:

I was going to call this my proud day, but that would have been for my pleasure, so it is instead PENANCE.

This was a proud day for me. You have always been everything I could ever wish for in a daughter, so I am writing the following just for you.

*If I have wronged you, dear, by what I have said or done, shirked my
duty in the race of your life before the race was done;*

*If I have lived a life in ease while you stood in need, have been a
stumbling block or missed a loving deed;*

*If I have ever failed to smile, and gave a frown instead, failed to try
to help relieve you of your dread;*

*If I have failed to speak a word of encouraging cheer, or failed you in
distress to relieve you of your fear;*

*If I was depressed and failed to see the sunlight of your love, too blind
to admit you are a blessing from above:*

Please, Daughter, Forgive.

Mother.
My penance to you.

I did not fully appreciate this letter from Mother when I was a
girl. But when I read it now, more than six decades later, I just cry at
the letter's power and emotion. It is overwhelming to me.

Chapter 7

Elvis and College

During the summer after high school graduation and before I went to college, I kept working in the family businesses. My brother was in charge, since, by this time, Daddy had shut down the radio show and moved to Florida. (He and Mother divorced in 1957, and then later remarried and divorced again.)

One day that summer, Bettye, Louis Jack's wife, asked me to go with her to meet Elvis at Dewey Phillips' radio station, WDIA, in the Chisca Hotel. Bettye was in the radio business, and she'd gotten word that Elvis was going to be there. Bettye and I drove there and arrived by early evening. When we walked in, Elvis was there, talking to Dewey. Elvis was clean shaven, his hair was nice, and he was well dressed. Lamar Fike, a close friend of Elvis, was also there. I knew him because he used to come to the Plantation Inn and Pancho's, and he knew Daddy and Louis Jack well. It was just the four of us. Elvis talked a lot, including to himself. Lamar had a polaroid, and Bettye asked if he would take pictures with us. He said "Yes."

I got a polaroid photo with Elvis—just Elvis and me, myself, and I. I was so happy. I was polaroid happy. Elvis had a huge smile, and, of course, mine was just as huge. It was almost as if we were doing a dental commercial.

After a little while, Elvis said, "Let's go to my house." Bettye and I agreed, and I was in the back seat with Lamar. Bettye was in the front with Elvis, who was driving. As we went down Union Ave., a car filled with girls pulled up next to us when he stopped at a red light. They were shouting, "Elvis, Elvis, Elvis." He nodded and smiled, and then took off when the light was green. For some reason, Bettye started singing Dave Gardner's *White Silver Sands*, and within a few minutes, Elvis told Bettye she had the lyrics wrong. Bettye must have been nervous to pick that song, much less try to sing it.

We arrived at Elvis's home on Audubon Drive—the one he lived in before Graceland. It was a nice ranch-style house. Elvis was kind to me. He escorted me to his den, which had a pool table, which I liked. We chatted for about ten minutes, mostly about pool and his mother, Gladys. Then he and Bettye went to another part of the house. Elvis said they were going to talk about the radio business, and he said they would not be long. He also said he would be back to check on me, and that his mother was in the kitchen if I needed anything.

After Elvis left, Gladys Presley came into the den and asked if I was OK. I said that I was and thanked her. Elvis had a phone next to the sofa so I called Billy and told him where I was. He didn't seem too happy that I was out so late in Memphis and hanging out at Elvis's place.

After a while, Bettye and Elvis reappeared, and it was time to get home. As we were driving back to West Memphis, Bettye told me that she had slept with Elvis. I didn't say anything—I just kept my mouth shut. She dropped me off at Mother's house, where I was living, and then she went to her home with Louis Jack, around the corner.

When I got home it was late—after 10:00 p.m. The next day Louis Jack called me to ask what had happened in Memphis, and I told him everything that happened except that Bettye told me she slept with Elvis. My brother bawled me out for staying out so late. But I didn't care since I got a photo taken with Elvis, and that was a big deal to me.

Unfortunately, I no longer have that cherished photo. I gave it to Daddy, who gave a copy to the West Memphis *Evening Times*, which ran the photo next to a story about Elvis leaving for the Army in March 1958. Daddy also had the picture blown up and hung in every Pancho's restaurant. I never got that photo back from Daddy, and I gave my only copy to Billy. I am very disappointed not to have that photo today. I hope one day to search old copies of the *Evening Times* to find that story.

I met Elvis just one more time. Through my brother Louis Jack, I had met George Klein, a Memphis DJ and a friend of Elvis. One day George called me and asked if I could get Gay Barfield, the girl who had succeeded me as Miss West Memphis, to meet him at Graceland and go on a date with him. I asked Gay, and she said, "Yes." George met us at the side door of Graceland, which entered a sitting area that opened up to a corridor of sofas. At the other end of the corridor was the living room with a piano.

Elvis was in the room with two girls. Introductions were made. Elvis was very kind but did not seem to remember me from my last visit. At some point Elvis got upset with one of the girls, who was flirting with him and dominating the conversation. We listened to Elvis play the piano and sing for about ten minutes. I left Gay with George, said goodbye, and left.

That fall, I left home, West Memphis, and my friends to go to college. I applied to the University of Mexico for art and also to

Southern Methodist University. But I chose the University of Miami. My family and I had visited Miami a lot, and I liked the weather and was familiar with the area. The University of Miami put me in touch with a girl from Memphis, Betty Bolton, who was also attending Miami that fall. Mother and Daddy drove me and Betty to Miami. Betty wanted to stay in the dorms at Miami instead of with her father, who lived down there. Mother arranged for that to happen, and Betty was so grateful.

Then Mother and Daddy visited Cuba after they dropped us off. Cuba at the time was a popular tourist destination—it had beautiful hotels and casinos, and great music. Mother and Daddy visited in the midst of the civil war there, when Fidel Castro's guerillas were challenging the government of Fulgencio Batista. So, it was an interesting time to be there. Mother said that government officials with machine-gun-toting bodyguards were everywhere. She didn't seem to care about that, but she did talk a lot about the fabulous layers of drapes in the suite at the hotel. There must have been at least six layers of drapes, she told me.

Meanwhile, I was officially a University of Miami Hurricane. In the fall semester I took Spanish, Art, Interior Design, and English. I went through rush and pledged Tri Delta—a great group of girls. One of the girls in my pledge class, Toni Thibodoux, would become a lifelong friend. Toni was from Lafayette, Louisiana. She was good looking, had a wild personality, and would keep you laughing constantly. We had a lot in common. She had grown up working in her family shoe business and had created a dance studio with her sister.

Halfway through the first semester, the Tri Delts developed a dance routine for a show we put on that was very creative. All of the girls were talented dancers. Our costumes were pajamas. I danced in the performance and was so happy because I had my music back. The President of Tri Delta was a girl from Cuba. She kept talking about Batista and Castro and seemed to favor Castro.

That fall I met Bill Hayes, a football player, in the library, where I studied. He was gorgeous. We were not sitting really close, but I clearly saw a very handsome, blue-eyed young man. We made eye contact for a good, long time. I later met him at a Sigma Nu fraternity party that the Tri Deltas attended. He asked me out to a fraternity get-together, and I accepted. I never told Billy about it, but nothing happened between us. We just ate, and he took me home to my dorm.

I stayed at the University of Miami for only one semester. I was a little homesick. I missed Billy a lot. Even though I had fun, I felt displaced. I couldn't concentrate on my studies. I cannot really explain why I left Miami beyond these reasons, but it just didn't feel right. And, so, at the end of the semester, I went home and dropped out of Miami to attend the Memphis Academy of Art.

About a month after I returned home, Billy asked me to marry him. We were at my house alone, in the living room, standing up. He pulled a ring out of his pocket—a platinum ring with a tiny diamond in the middle that he had bought with his own money from jobs he had surveying land. And then he said: "Will you marry me?"

I was shocked and didn't say "Yes" right away. I was hyperventi-lating—both excited and frightened. In a way, it was my dream come true, since I had always loved Billy so much. But I also viewed marriage as a form of confinement, like the other forms of confinement I had grown up with. When I composed myself, I said "Yes, I will marry you." I loved Billy; he was everything I wanted. Or so I felt at the time.

Soon after Billy and I were engaged, the phone rang at Mother's house and it was Gladys Presley, Elvis's Mother. Elvis had seen me in a television ad for Pancho's. Gladys asked Mother if I would go out on a date with him. Mother declined in a nice way on my behalf. How Gladys got our telephone number, I don't know. I wasn't too upset about not going on a date with Elvis, believe it or not, because I was in love with Billy.

However, over the next few months, doubts started to enter my mind about Billy. He wanted a country, laid-back life that he loved. When I would think about marrying him, I felt my throat closing because I would be confined for the rest of my life. That was like a death sentence for me. I came to see marriage to Billy as a form of control over my life, akin to the control that my mother had always exercised over me.

For the next year or so, I attended the Memphis Academy of Arts and studied decorating. Billy and I continued to date, but we never talked about a wedding date, since, after college, Billy went into the military. I wanted more independence from my family, and, so, I got a part-time job in West Memphis as a secretary at the Goodyear Tire Company. I don't remember much about this period, except that I was living life day to day.

Chapter 8

Jack Goldsmith, Jr.

A t about this point, sometime in 1960, my world turned upside down, sideways, vertical, and horizontal.

The phone rang in Mother's house, and she answered it. The voice said, "This is Jack Goldsmith. May I speak to Brenda Berger?" Mother said, "No, you dirty old man." And she hung up the phone and left it off the hook.

Mother had made a mistake. She thought the call was from Jack Goldsmith, *Sr.*, the owner of the famous *Goldsmith's* Department Store in Memphis. It was actually from his seventeen-year-old son, Jack *Jr.* I later learned that Jack had heard about me from his father's mistress, Mickey, who was a friend of Bettye Berger's.

About two hours later, there was a knock on the door. It was Jack Jr. Mother went to the door, and I was listening from the hall. "I think there is something wrong with your phone," he said, as he politely marched past Mother into the dining area and found the phone off the hook. He told Mother he would really like to meet me.

With that I emerged into the dining room. Jack was very handsome. He was in great shape. He had slightly slanted, beautiful brown eyes, and charming facial expressions. He was very well dressed. I was immediately drawn to him for his energy, boldness, and good looks.

As Mother looked on, Jack told me he would like to take me to a polo match in Germantown in Memphis. I told him I would like that, since I had never been to a polo match. I said I would go if he would give me a little time to change clothes. I could tell that Mother was annoyed. She stayed very quiet. I was in control, but I wasn't in control—and I kind of liked it. Here was a handsome stranger who arrived from nowhere and was courting me *despite* my mother's wishes.

I agreed to go on a date with Jack Jr., even though I was engaged to Billy, who was in the National Guard and out of town. I had no idea what I was doing. I was taken with Jack Jr.'s energy and was mesmerized by his controlling personality. He had come to my house even though my mother had told him off on the telephone, and he somehow got my address and walked into my house without asking for permission. And then he got a date with me right off the bat. He was a smooth operator, and he did a number on me.

I changed clothes, and Jack and I went outside and got in his father's Jaguar convertible. As we drove away, Jack started talking in a random way about himself and his family, and I just listened. He first complained that I was hard to get ahold of. And then he started talking about his family in a derogatory way. Next, he talked about polo. He said he was a polo player and an instructor. He talked about his nice house in Germantown. And then he started talking about the girls he had dated and how he was sick of them, and how he had decided to start a new life with me. This was shocking and hard to process. Jack was very bold, very to-the-point, and very full of himself.

We never made it to the polo match. As we got over the bridge in Memphis, he said it might be too late for polo, and asked if I'd like some ice cream. I said, "Yes." He took us to his favorite place in Germantown. The ice cream was delicious. From there, we drove to the nearby polo grounds, where the game was breaking up. I missed the game, but it was exciting to see polo players for the first time.

Jack said he wanted to show me where his mother and father lived. As we drove, he discussed Culver Military Academy in Indiana, where he went to school and played polo. You could tell he loved the game. He told me about the other sports he played. And then, as if it were no big deal, he told me he had sex with the head Colonel's daughter and got caught. "They kicked me out of school, but my father made sure I graduated," he told me.

We pulled into his mother's drive, which was in a setting of beautiful trees in the woods, down a winding hill. She was out of town. We pulled up to a cottage adjacent to the house, his bachelor pad, which was near a swimming pool. He said he would show me around, but he worried his mother might show up. So, we turned and went one street over to his father's place, a beautiful mansion that Fred Smith of Federal Express would later purchase.

Jack next drove by the Jewish Community Center and Memphis' premiere golf course, Greenbrier. He asked if I would like to play with him the next day. I said I had never played golf. He said he would teach me. I said OK. On the way home he returned to the topic of his family. He said he despised his mother and that his father had just married a lady with two boys who were a little younger than him. He did not like his father's new wife and resented the boys because his father had adopted them. I just listened and tried to absorb his pain.

So went my first date, learning about Jack Goldsmith, Jr. He dropped me off at Mother's house. He got out of the car and walked me to the house. We said goodbye without kissing.

My mind was blown by the experience. I had never had a day like that in my life. It was so much fun. I saw so many new and exciting things, and I had met this very smart, handsome, worldly, free-spirited young man with a wild past. When I got home, I didn't think one bit about Billy. Strangely, Mother did not ask me about my day with Jack when I got home.

Jack arrived the next morning to pick me up for golf. He asked me to bring a swimsuit in case we wanted to go swimming. *Oh me, oh my*, this worried me. I knew the swimming pool was next to his bachelor pad, and I wondered if he would try to take advantage of me.

We drove to Germantown, and I played golf for the first time. Jack seemed to relax more on the golf course and did not rattle on about his life. This made me more relaxed, and I enjoyed the new sport even though I wasn't great. He was kind and taught me how to swing. As we teed off on one hole, he pointed to the back of his father's house with a huge swimming pool and cabana.

He got bored with golf after a few holes, and, so, we went to his mother's house and his bachelor pad. Jack showed me where to go to change into my swimsuit and told me to meet him at the pool. I had brought the only swimsuit I could find, which was my mother's, since I did not have one.

As I changed, I was surrounded by an upscale Ralph Lauren-decorated interior for a grown-up Prince. I emerged in Mother's swimsuit and stood on the side of the pool, wondering what to do next. "Where did you get that ugly swimsuit?" he said. I was angry and in shock. I knew it was not sexy, but I also knew it fit me, and it was all I had to wear. I did not go swimming. I went back into his place and put my clothes back on. That was the last time I was ever there.

I came out and waited for him to go in and change clothes. Together we went to the car as if nothing had happened. I never mentioned how rude he was. He drove me down to the end of his mother's street and showed me acres of land that were on the market, divided into lots. He pulled over and said, "How do you like it?" It was undeveloped dirt lots with a few trees. "Once they start building, it should be nice," I said. Then we drove away and headed back to get more ice cream.

On the way, he asked how I would like to live on the land he showed me. I did not give him an answer as I did not know where he was coming from. Then Jack took me home. That was our second date.

Several days later, we went on our third date. Thank goodness Billy was somewhere in Oklahoma. This time Jack asked me to go fishing at his father's cabin on Horseshoe Lake. My quick answer was: "What day and what time?" I asked, because I was working the graveyard shift at Pancho's, and I did not finish until 8:00 a.m. Jack suggested 7:00 a.m. I told him I could not go then, and why. He agreed to pick me up at 8:00 a.m. at Pancho's.

The next morning, he drove up in a different car with two people in it. Jack introduced me to his father's mistress, Mickey, and her daughter. That is the way he said it. This was my first meeting with a mistress and a mistress's daughter. She was a brunette, nice-looking, and kind. Mickey started talking about how she and my brother's wife, Bettye Berger, met and how long they had known each other.

Jack was quiet until we got to the cotton fields along the road to Horseshoe Lake. He started laughing and said, "I should take this car across the fields like I did with my grandmother Tommy." Jack was very close to Tommy, his mother's mother. He told the story about how she wanted a new car from his father and took the one she had over the cotton fields until it ruined the bottom. The maneuver worked:

Tommy got a brand-new car after telling Jack Sr. that the car was falling apart and putting his son in danger. Jack loved telling this story, but, at this point, his spoiled personality was starting to bother me.

We arrived at the entrance of Horseshoe Lake. On the right, there was a store for snacks and fishing tackle. On the left was the long wooden pier for pole- and fly-fishing. And to the left of the pier, along the lakefront, was a dirt road that took us to his father's cabin. It looked lovely on the outside, and the part facing the lake had a large screened-in porch.

We piled out of the car and followed Jack to the door. He tried to open the door, but it was locked. He did not have a key. So, what did he do? The frustrated Prince immediately broke into the house through the front door by ramming it with his foot several times. I didn't know how to comprehend this. Here was someone who seemed together but suddenly was embarrassed and lost his temper and his control. I didn't like it.

From this point, Jack had lost his grip on his emotions. He showed us around the house, and then said, "Let's take a walk." We followed him to the pier and walked out to where the boat was covered under an open boathouse. He crawled into the boat for a few seconds and then pointed out at the lake and told the story of how he saved two boys from drowning in the lake. My disappointment in Jack faded a bit when he was telling the story. But not for long.

He got out of the boat and walked back to the cabin. He was still agitated. Back in the house, we discovered there was no food and no bait. Jack lost his temper again and said, "This is not working." The house was not stocked in the way he was used to, and, rather than do something about it, Jack decided we would just go home. I was agitated, but I felt bad for Jack.

And, so, we left the cabin without securing the door. We arrived at my mother's house in West Memphis and made no plans for future dates. Jack had to go college, to the University of Tennessee. Several days later, I received a letter from Jack which began: "My roommate is writing this letter for me." Jack had dictated the letter. I was really turned off by this. I thought he was lazy and consumed with talking and thinking excessively about himself because of an undue sense of his self-importance. The letter basically said that he was in school and would see me soon.

Chapter 9

My (First) Marriage to Jack

As things slowed down a bit with Jack, I got a call from Billy asking me to visit him in Oklahoma. I agreed. By this point, I was starting to question whether I should continue my engagement. I had had three dates with Jack, and, by comparison, Billy seemed a little dull. I was changing and maturing, and starting to think I wanted more than to spend my life in West Memphis. I still cared about Billy, but I was overpowered by Jack.

Billy's pal's girlfriend called and asked if she could go with me to Oklahoma. I was happy to have someone to talk to during the drive. When we arrived, the two boys had a motel room for us. Billy and I had no time alone, so I could not tell him about Jack and about how my feelings toward Billy were changing.

Basically, all we did was stay in the motel room, all four lying on the bed talking and kissing and holding each other so tight there was no air. I felt Billy's body and heart and love, but I was resistant for some reason. I disliked the confinement in there, just as I had always disliked confinement in West Memphis. I did not see any of the town except for driving in and out. And that was the end of the Oklahoma date with Billy.

When I got home, Mother decided that she and I needed to take a short vacation to Hot Springs, Arkansas, for a few days. Just before we left, Jack called, and I told him I was leaving town. When I got to Hot Springs, there was a floral arrangement in the hotel. The weird thing about the arrangement was the card. The card read, "I love you. I am in St. Louis. Jack." It was written in the same distinctive handwriting as Jack had used on the envelope on the letter from college.

I saved the card and still have it to this day. I have no idea how that card got to Hot Springs to be delivered with those flowers. It is still a mystery. I wondered if Jack was in Hot Springs. I was in a weird limbo. I knew I was losing interest in Billy, and Jack managed to communicate with me in a way I found exciting.

A few days later, back in West Memphis, Jack showed up one fall evening in 1961 at my house. He said he had heard the Ray Charles song "Hit the Road, Jack" while in college, and he did. He went to New York after skipping out of college. His mother and father had a private detective find him. "But I made friends with him, I paid him off, and we had a ball," Jack told me.

The detective accompanied Jack back to Memphis, and now he was at my door. Jack updated me on what he had been doing and then returned to college. He also said he hoped I would come visit him in Knoxville. Perhaps I should have been mad that Jack showed up briefly and then left, but I wasn't. I was just happy to see him and looking forward to Knoxville.

Within a week, Jack called. He told me he had gonorrhea and asked me to call Andrew to tell him to make him a doctor's appointment in Memphis for first thing in the morning. Andrew was Jack Sr.'s chauffeur, and the person Jack Jr. was closest to in the world. Andrew practically raised Jack Jr. when he was a boy, when his parents owned and lived in the Gayoso hotel in Memphis. Jack's father was too busy with his work and his mistress to be a good father to him. And his mother was an alcoholic and abusive. They left it to Andrew to raise Jack. He was like Bertha, a good friend and partner. But he also introduced Jack to many vices—including gambling and prostitutes—at a very young age.

I don't know why, but something in my life prevented me from thinking things through. I perhaps should have been appalled or worried that Jack had gonorrhea. I knew it had something to do with sex. But I missed the bigger picture. I told Mother about it, and she did not fill in the picture for me.

I called Andrew, as Jack asked. (I'm not sure why Jack didn't call Andrew himself). I also agreed to meet Jack at the airport when his flight arrived from Knoxville. Mother came with me. In those days there was just a tiny building for the airport so you could park the car and see everyone coming out. Jack came out on time, met us, and asked if he could borrow our car to visit the doctor the next day. When Mother said, "Yes," he dropped Mother and me off at our house and left. He brought the car back the next day after his doctor's visit. He said he was OK and that Andrew was taking him back to the airport so he could get back to school.

Soon Jack invited me to come to Knoxville to visit him, as he had promised. He said he would buy me a plane ticket for Knoxville. "I will pick you up at the airport and get a room for you," he said. *Freedom at last*, I thought. But the alert button came on in my mind: *I have to get someone to go with me to protect me from Jack and the motel room.*

Jack had been a gentleman during our relationship to that point, but, because of my past nightmares, I believed I had to protect myself from men. And even though I did not understand the full implications of what he told me about his gonorrhea, I understood enough to know that Jack was sexually experienced, and that made me cautious. Billy was the only one I could trust without feeling fear and preparing for the worst.

The friend who accompanied me to Knoxville was Ann Cline, a friend from Miss Lee's School. But Ann called at the last second to say something had come up and that she would have to take the next plane. So, when I landed in Knoxville, I was alone. Jack was on the tarmac with a huge bouquet of flowers. (This was the second bouquet from Jack, but I never really liked flowers). Jack did not kiss or hug me, but he said he was glad I was there.

It was late in the afternoon, and he drove to the motel. It took forever to get there. We passed motel after motel. I asked if he knew where he was going. He said he knew the area well. Then came the jolt. "I have been to every motel on this highway with a girl, and I did not want to take you to the same motel," he said. "I wanted you to have one that I had not had a girl in."

Wow. Good thing I'd grown up in the nightclub. Never, ever think that you have heard it all until you hear it all. Anyway, I admired Jack's honesty. When he first met me, Jack told me that he wanted someone unlike the girls he had been with. I was a different kind of girl than he was used to, and he was looking for something different in his life. But he didn't really know how to deal with me.

We finally arrived at the motel. Jack dropped me off and said he would see me later after picking up Ann. Thank goodness, I could relax. It seemed like forever before Ann arrived. I had nothing to do but smoke and wait. My smoking habit began at the Plantation Inn, during the daytime, when I was alone, and Daddy left his Camel cigarettes on the sink in the bathroom. Being alone is very dangerous for me, I discovered as time went by.

Anyway, I opened the drawer by the bed and got out the Bible. I started reading passages. The clock seemed as if it were not ticking. Finally, around midnight, there was a knock on the door. It was Jack with Ann. Jack asked if we needed anything and said he would pick us up at 9:00 a.m.

Jack picked us up, and the three of us had a great day together. Jack took us to a beautiful view of the Tennessee River. I am sure Jack had a love for the spot he chose to take me on this trip, since he loved to fish, and it was known for great bass fishing. We then had lunch and had a light conversation. Jack said he had some friends he wanted me to meet. They were coming into Memphis to visit him. He then drove us back to the airport, and we flew home.

A few weeks later, Jack said he would like to pick me up in West Memphis and drive me to Nashville for a date. We stayed in a motel in separate rooms. The next day, Jack and I walked around Nashville. It was a beautiful day in October. We walked to the Capitol and climbed the steps. He held my hand for the first time, which was nice. On the way down, we sat down and looked out at the view.

As we were quietly absorbing the view, Jack took my hand and said, "Will you marry me?" I was engaged to one person, and another person was asking me to marry him. I definitely did not have my feet on solid ground with relationships. I was floating through life, being guided by a force that was not me but that had taken hold of me.

I said, "Yes." I still had Billy in my heart and soul. And yet the draw of freedom and a strange infatuation was much more appealing than the strangulation of boredom and being stuck in one place for the rest of my life. Jack knew my feelings and that I was engaged to Billy.

He said he would take me away, and we would be happy. That was all I wanted—to be taken away. Later in life, I wrote a song called "The Gypsy in My Soul." I felt like I had gypsy blood, and Jack did, too.

Jack and I were on a fast track. We actually had a lot in common. We both had Jewish fathers and gentile mothers. Both of our fathers owned retail stores. We were both isolated as children, since we lived in our parents' adult world and never really had close childhood friends. We were both spoiled in our own way. And we were both desperate to get away from our families.

Jack and I drove from Nashville to Memphis as soon as we were engaged. We still had not kissed. On the drive, I started getting nervous. The reality of what I had done was starting to take effect, like a bad meal. The love of my life was going to be hurt and let down.

Jack dropped me off at Mother's in West Memphis and returned to Memphis. I told Mother that I was engaged. She was speechless. She did not congratulate me or hug me. She just went about her business as usual, as if nothing had happened. I suspected that she was upset because she didn't want me with any man, and she wanted me at home, near her. But she never explained or complained.

I called Billy and told him that we would not be engaged or married or even in the same town. He was very quiet. I'd hurt someone for the first time in my life, and I still feel bad about it to this day.

Jack made arrangements pretty quickly for the marriage. "We are going to Trenton, Georgia, to get married," he told me the next day. I asked, "Why?" He said that an eighteen-year-old like him needed parental consent to be married in Tennessee. "Georgia is the nearest state to accept my age for marriage," Jack said.

At that point, I told my father about the engagement and that we were getting married in Trenton. Daddy clearly was not happy. He insisted that he and Louis Jack—who also wasn't pleased—drive with us to Trenton. Daddy wanted to make sure that Jack and I did not consummate our relationship before marriage. Jack did not object, but he wasn't really excited about it.

Mother was sad and did not want to go with us. So, Jack, Daddy, Louis Jack, and I got into Louis Jack's Oldsmobile in the late evening and took off. Louis Jack drove; Jack and I were in the back seat. Jack was clearly nervous during the drive. I was excited but had no idea what the future held.

We drove all night and arrived in Trenton on the morning of November 4, 1961—our wedding day. Jack had done his homework. He told Louis Jack where to park and then got out and walked me into a jewelry store on the corner to get my wedding ring. I must say he was very impressive at that point. He seemed to have everything planned. Jack picked out a ring—a wedding band with no stone. He asked if I liked it, and I said I did. Jack seemed so excited.

After he got the ring, we walked to the courthouse. We got a marriage license there—there was no waiting period—and went to a judge's chambers. My marriage outfit was a cropped soft wool beige full coat and pants that I had bought in Memphis several months earlier. My dream wedding dress was in a scrapbook at home—beautiful white lace. I had put it there when I was 13. My dreams never became a reality, but I will never stop dreaming.

The judge had a very loud, very southern drawl. "We are gathered here with Jack Landman Goldsmith, Jr. and Brenda Lou Berger to join them in marriage," he said. A few minutes later, I became Brenda Goldsmith. My life was moving very fast. I had just started on a new path that would bring me the three most beautiful gifts—my three sons. For that I will always feel blessed. But my immediate future was in the hands of Jack Jr. We ate lunch and drove home, arriving near sundown.

When we arrived in West Memphis, Mother and I hugged. Jack and I agreed to stay in the house overnight. Mother went to her bedroom and Daddy stayed in the living room on the sofa. He told Jack he did not want us to consummate the marriage until Jack's parents approved the marriage. He feared that they would somehow have the marriage annulled, and he wanted me to stay a virgin—just in case.

But after Daddy had gone to sleep, Jack wanted to have sex. I had an iron bed and any movement it made a loud squeak. Jack was cussing and frustrated. He took me by the hand and said, "Come on—we are going to the bathroom." He laid me down on the floor and asked me to move the scales that were on the floor. I thought he said that we would need the scales and asked why. Jack got very frustrated. It was a small bathroom, and we were both uncomfortable, exhausted, and emotionally drained. We went back to my room without having sex.

The next morning Jack said he was going to Memphis, and he asked me to meet him at the Gayoso Hotel, which his father owned and where he had once lived. "We are going to have a honeymoon, and no one will be looking over their shoulder at us," he said. So, I packed a bag and met him at the Gayoso Hotel.

Jack pointed out places that were important to him as a child growing up. He told me what it was like growing up in the hotel and said he had a whole floor of the hotel devoted to sports. As a child, he could go to Goldsmith's department store, next door, anytime he liked and get whatever toy or sports equipment he wanted. But he had to play by himself—all of his friends were in East Memphis and he was stuck downtown at the hotel.

The time had come for us to consummate our marriage. Jack had arranged a room. Next to my side of the bed was a package of condoms. He asked that I hand him one. (Years later, I wondered why there was a package of condoms there. It made me think this was where Jack brought all of his girls.)

My first experience with sex was weird. I felt like I may have missed something. Jack just satisfied himself, got dressed, and left, telling me to meet him in the Men's Department at Goldsmith's. Then I discovered something I did not know—one of the weirdest experiences of my life. Blood was on the bed. I was very naïve. I had no idea where the blood came from but later found out it came from me. I had preserved my virginity for this one night, and it was over with in a flash.

The episode took me back to Billy at the drive-in movies. We would make out and then he would have to get out of the car and push the car. I asked him what he was doing, and he said releasing tension, his sexual pain. If I had known how quickly you lose your virginity, I might not have saved it for marriage. It seems really stupid to me. I also came to think, after a few more marriages, that the piece of paper establishing a marriage is meaningless.

I met Jack at Goldsmith's, as he had asked. I didn't love entering the huge department store alone to meet my new husband. I was following orders but didn't know what was happening. When I saw Jack, he had a smile on his face and looked so handsome. He took me to meet his father in his office at Goldsmith's. Jack Sr. was very nice. He was understanding and even-keeled, and gave us advice about marriage. No one else seemed happy, though. My new marriage to Jack displeased my parents. Louis Jack seemed jealous. And Billy was devastated. Jack's mother, Geneva, who was an alcoholic, was the most upset of all. I later found out she said I robbed her son from the cradle. But Jack's grandmother, Tommy, seemed pleased with our marriage.

Jack and me, soon after our marriage

I met Jack's mother, Geneva, the Christmas after we were married, in her apartment in downtown Memphis. She had gray hair pulled back tight in a bun. We sat in the kitchen. She gave me Christmas gifts. The first one was horrible-looking. It was a maid's dress that was too large for me. The second present was a fur coat. It was beautiful and fit me. Geneva was playing games with me by giving me an ugly dress and a gorgeous coat.

Jack and I lived in West Memphis at Mother's home. We started receiving wedding gifts—money, pots and pans, silver pieces, and crystal. We started to talk about our future and decided to move to Florida, where I would go back to the University of Miami and Jack would get a job and attend Miami as well. I knew I had to face my future as it came—and it was coming fast. I felt Jack's love, but only in spurts, since he was absorbed in himself and his world.

While we were making plans for Florida, we went to spend an evening at Jack Sr.'s house in Memphis. Mother came with us. Jack Sr.'s wife Dorothy was there, as was Jack's half-sister Joan, who was wonderful and said great things about me. Joan brought her daughter Cheryl, an adorable three-year old.

We congregated in the breakfast nook. It was adjacent to a beautiful den of blue oriental designs—distinguished and impressive. Jack Sr. again congratulated us and gave an old-fashioned speech about how to have a happy and good marriage. He also congratulated my mother for being a great customer and having a great loan record at the First Tennessee Bank, where he was on the board. On the whole, the evening went well.

Before we left for Florida, and while staying at Mother's house, Jack brought out a deck of cards and asked if we wanted to play poker. Mother was happy with that. But soon she started cheating by trying to pass me a card. Jack caught her. He went into a tirade and threw his cards on the table and lost it. I had never heard such an outburst. It was a nightmare, because he reminded me of my father when he was drunk, and that was scary. Thank goodness that was the first and last time I ever saw him get like that. He was usually easygoing and happy-go-lucky. I would cling to the Jack that I knew and not the horrible-tirade action figure that I just experienced.

One morning in December of 1961, we left for Florida in my car, which was a Chevrolet convertible that Mother had given me. We packed up the car, along with money, some of our gifts, and a few pieces of luggage and hit the road. On our way to Florida, we stopped in Nashville for the evening. We went to Printers Alley. Jack ordered a Jack Daniels and Coke and ordered me one, too. I had never had a drink in my life. Our nightclub smelled like liquor in the daytime, and I always hated the smell.

I took a sip and did not like it, so, I put sugar in the Jack Daniels. Big mistake. By the time we got to the hotel, I was sick. I threw up and threw up. Jack was wonderful. He got me into a shower and helped me get my body back to normal again. I really felt like he was there for me and did not put me down at all.

On our way down the highway in Florida toward Miami late one night, a heavy fog descended. Jack had to drive very slowly because we could not see anything except, at some point, a huge bright shining light. Jack stopped the car and an officer appeared. He told us to stop driving until the fog cleared because it was too dangerous. I cuddled up next to Jack and we were quiet, sitting in the fog. It was nice.

We arrived in North Miami Beach a few days later. We checked in at the Castaways hotel. It had a great theme. Built on two sites, the ocean and the intracoastal, it had an island atmosphere, a nightclub, fun music, and a young crowd. It was better because we were on our own, away from our parents, and both relaxed. I think I got pregnant with my first child at the Castaways.

Jack's father got him a part time job at Burdine's Department Store. And after a few days of looking around the University of Miami, we found a new furnished apartment—a one-bedroom not far from the University.

Within about six weeks, I got deathly nauseated. I made an appointment to see a gynecologist. I was pregnant. Every morning I would get sick when I smelled cigarette smoke from Jack. The smoke seemed to penetrate any room I was in. When we drove around town Jack would light up in our convertible thinking all would be well, but still, I would get sick. The Coral Gables wind didn't disperse the smoke; it passed it right under my nose.

In addition to working at Burdine's and attending the University of Miami, Jack made a connection with a waterski manufacturer in Mexico. He got money from his father to start a business distributing the skis to boat and ski companies in the Miami area and up the coast. Jack would stop by dealers up and down Federal highway. He was a great salesman and a great exaggerator. He made lots of sales. Unfortunately for Jack, all of the money he invested did not bring in a penny. When the skis arrived at the airport from Mexico they were warped because the plane was not properly insulated. So, Jack's first great idea to make money did not work out.

One day I noticed Jack standing in our front yard, talking to two girls. This happened more than once. It bothered me because he was flirting. It also bothered me that we went to a big boat show in Coral Gables, supposedly to sell skis, when in fact Jack wanted to flirt with the women in bikinis. I started to feel like a third wheel.

About that time, I found a yellow discharge on Jack's underwear. This upset me, but I did not allow myself to fully register where it came from or what it meant. I was in a "never, ever" state of mind, avoiding the reality of the situation. We made a doctor's appointment for Jack. I did not go to the doctor with him; he was on his own. He acted as if everything was OK when he came home.

Chapter 10

First Divorce
and Second Marriage

When I found out I was pregnant, I called Mother. She and Bertha drove to Florida. When they arrived, Mother and Bertha both hugged me. "Brenda, you look beautiful," Mother said. "And Jack, you look horrible." Jack was stressed and probably still suffering from the sex infection.

Mother and Bertha got a room and rested. The next day, we showed them our apartment. Then the four of us rode around the neighborhoods, looking for a small house in a new development. After a few hours, Mother suggested that we come back to West Memphis. She said she would give us the land adjacent to her residence and help us finance a home on that property. A few months earlier I could not wait to leave West Memphis. But now, after just three months in Florida, I was ready to return after Mother made her offer. I wanted Mother and Bertha's help with getting through the pregnancy and with a new baby.

So, Jack and I quit school, he quit his job, and we took off for home. While the house in West Memphis was being designed and built, we stayed in a new apartment in a building in Memphis that Jack Sr. owned. On September 26, 1962, I checked into Baptist Hospital. And before I knew it, I was the mother of a fighting, boxing baby boy, Jack Landman Goldsmith III, whom we called "Little Jack."

When we got back to Memphis, Jack started a new business with money his father loaned him. He bought several bubble-gum machines and huge, expensive vending machines. The first vending machines went into Goldsmith's. Jack rented a small storefront on Poplar Avenue to store equipment and supplies. At night, Jack would check on his machines around town to empty the money out of them. I surmised at the time that he was also visiting women during his nights out.

When Jack checked on the vending machines at Goldsmith's, he would also "shop" there. He simply grabbed what he wanted and left. I once asked him why he did this. He sloughed it off as if it was not a big deal, since he had done this all his life.

One night, Jack told me to look in Little Jack's closet. It was full of the sexiest, most revealing lingerie that Goldsmith's had. It wasn't my style, and wearing it made me very uncomfortable. I was becoming aware that Jack wanted me to be something I wasn't—a sex object. I had been anxious about Jack's flirtations and evidence of his liaisons with others. But now he seemed to be targeting me. I realized at this point that things were not right in our marriage.

About this time, I met Jack's half-sister Joan downtown for lunch. She warned me that I had a difficult future with Jack. "He is a nice boy, but he will give you a lot of heartache," she said. "And so will my crazy family, especially Geneva," Jack's alcoholic mother. I sensed that Joan was right. And although it did not make me happy, I liked her very much for her honesty.

Some nights Jack would come home with huge bags of coins from his vending machines. He would empty the bags on our bedspread. Then we would separate and count the money. The bubble gum machines collected only pennies, which Jack wanted to go through to see if we could find a rare coin that might be valuable. So, we counted and separated pennies with Little Jack lying next to us on a clean blanket to give him a little protection from the filthy coins. The experience brought me back in time to my counting with Mother all the money that came in from our businesses.

On September 26, 1963, Little Jack had his first birthday. In the living room we had a playpen, where he stayed during the day and would pull himself up and jabber away. Bertha told me that he was going to walk on his birthday. And sure enough, he did. Bertha loved Little Jack so much. When he walked that day, she just said, "I knew he would, I just knew he would," grinning with her pretty smile.

Jack Jr. and Jack III

We moved into a larger apartment that Jack Sr. also owned. At about this time Jack asked to take polaroid photos of me in the nude. I hated the idea. It was like asking me to walk down Broadway in West Memphis naked. Jack wanted what he wanted and did not respect my wishes. He insisted and insisted until I gave in. I was miserably unhappy at that point, except for having my son.

One day in November of 1963, I was in the car with Little Jack and I was talking to Mother on our car phone—a radio-based phone that many people used back then. After that call, I picked up the phone to call someone else and heard Jack's voice on the other end of the phone. I guess his car phone was on the same frequency as my car phone. Anyway, he was talking to a girl I had once worked with, and it was not small talk. I was listening to things that were cutting through my soul. When he said, "Don't worry about Brenda," my life crumbled.

It seemed to take forever for Jack to arrive home. I confronted him with what I heard. He didn't get upset. He remained cool and did not respond. I was not happy at all and was ready to scream. We didn't talk the rest of the day, and, that night, I stayed as far away from him as I could in the bed.

The next day was Thanksgiving and I had planned a nice meal. Bertha was helping me because I was pregnant, and the doctor wanted me to have bed rest, since I had had a miscarriage a few months earlier. Bertha put most of the food on the table and left some in the kitchen. When Bertha was out of the room, Jack asked for more turkey.

I had not gotten over my rage. I got up, and, contrary to doctor's orders, picked up the large tray and brought it to him. He asked for something else as I was approaching. I asked if he remembered the doctor's orders, which were not orders to cater to him. "You are so spoiled you can't even get your own food," I said. And then with the tray in my hand, I lifted up my leg, kicked him in the chest, handed him the tray of turkey, and turned around and went to my room.

A few days later, I had my second miscarriage. I think God meant them for a reason since I may have contracted something from Jack that may have affected the babies. By this point I was at the end of my rope. The road had come to an end. I was hurt beyond healing. Cheating is not something a person can forgive or forget. I was emotionally drained.

I took Little Jack and went to Mother's for the evening to rest after my miscarriage. After a few days, I decided I wanted a divorce. Jack helped me make up my mind when, the next day, I found him in bed with someone else in our apartment. They both jumped out the window like lightning. There was nothing left in my body to hurt. I was numb. I called Jack Sr. and told him I was moving out and that he could have his apartment back. I told him why.

I did not want to stay at Mother's because my brother would repeatedly tell me how wrong I was to have married Jack, and I did not need that. I needed my own space. I found a place in Memphis perfect for me and Little Jack, across from the Helen Shop on Union Avenue in Memphis. The apartment was on the third floor and beautiful. There were two bedrooms—one for Little Jack and one for me. Within a couple of weeks, Jack sent flowers and a card. "I am sorry, and I love you so much," he said. I hate flowers to this day. They seem to be a convenient gift to say anything you want, and they ruin the true beauty of a gift. The flowers did not deter me from getting a divorce.

Jack moved into a high-rise apartment building in the heart of the medical center in Memphis, near the Baptist Hospital where Little

Jack was born. The building was owned by his father and uncle, and other family members, and Jack had an ownership share as well.

Jack wanted to see Little Jack and asked if Bertha could bring him by. I agreed. Bertha was afraid to ride the elevator, so I went on it with her. We punched the elevator button on the ground floor just as it was closing, and Jack Jr. was inside when it opened. We didn't say a word to one another as the elevator ascended, but he looked at me as if he was going to eat me up. I was dressed in a white cashmere sweater and long white leggings. Bertha, Jack, and Little Jack got out on the floor of Jack's apartment. I picked Bertha up a few hours later. She said the visit was nice for a while, but Jack left the apartment after an hour.

Jack did not show up for or contest the divorce, which became official on March 29, 1965. I received custody of Little Jack. I also received Jack Jr.'s ownership share of the high-rise apartments near the medical center. The divorce decree obligated Jack to make alimony payments out of his trust fund.

One afternoon, just a few days after the divorce, I was at my Aunt Opal's house in West Memphis with Mother. Aunt Opal knew Billy Smith, my first love. Unbeknownst to me, she invited him over. When I saw him outside, I went out to greet him and gave him a big hug. I had missed him and was happy to see him. Right then and there Billy asked me to marry him. He said he had always loved me and would take care of me and Little Jack. I was shocked. I still had feelings for Billy. But I didn't want to marry him. I had the same thought as before: I wanted to get out of West Memphis, but Billy wanted to live there. "I'm just so sorry—I can't," I said. "Too much has happened."

Billy understood. A few months later, after I had remarried Jack Jr., I saw Billy at the West Memphis dog track, and he told me he had met an airline stewardess and was thinking about marrying her. I was blown away but wished him well. I later learned that he got out of West Memphis and moved to northern Florida to be a football coach. If I had known he was willing to leave West Memphis, I might have married him. Maybe I should have asked him that question when he asked me to marry him after the divorce.

Just a few weeks after Jack and I divorced, he called me. He said he loved me and told me he was in a psychiatric facility in New Canaan, Connecticut. He said he was seeing a psychiatrist, who had advised him that I was the only good thing in his life; that he should get back together with me; and that we should leave our families in Memphis and go far away, perhaps to New Mexico. "I need you, Brenda. Without you, I am nothing," he said.

I listened and told him I had been through too much with him and could not do it a second time. A couple of days later, I answered a knock on my apartment door. It was Jack with flowers in his hands—he never figured out that I didn't like flowers. I was very numb. But I let him in. He made the same pitch in the apartment as he had on the phone: about his mental condition, how he wanted to correct his life, how he needed me, and how we should move our family to New Mexico.

I still refused to give in. I was waiting for him to apologize, and to explain how we could possibly live together in light of his need for women outside our marriage. This concern was reinforced when he told me about the weekend trips from Connecticut that he took to New York, where he had a date with a girl who looked like Shirley MacLaine. *What a jerk*, I thought. With his speech over, Jack left empty-handed. He looked like a puppy dog that could not find his way home. I felt bad for him, but I had to protect me and my son.

But Jack did not give up. He returned to my apartment and told me that his psychiatrist would like to talk to me. He also said that the World's Fair was starting in New York, and that Little Jack would love it. "It will be a nice trip for the three of us," he said. I relented. I don't exactly know why, but I think it was because I needed Little Jack to have a father and because Jack was very convincing about turning over a new leaf.

So, the three of us took off in Jack's convertible MG for the World's Fair. We had lots of fun as a family, and I realized that I still loved Jack despite everything I had been through.

I met the doctor in Connecticut, who seemed professional and sincere. He said that Jack needed me, that we needed each other, and that this would work out for us. He also suggested that we move to New Mexico, where he was from. He said it was a nice place to live and far from our families. I put my faith into what the doctor had to say. And I remembered and was influenced by my mother's experiences sticking by my father's side no matter how many women he had. How she did this was beyond me, or maybe it wasn't.

So, Jack and I decided to remarry and move to Santa Fe. On the drive home, Jack said he wanted to return to Trenton, Georgia, for a repeat of "Dearly Beloved." Don't ask me why. On May 3, 1965—just five weeks after our divorce—Little Jack sat quietly on a bench in the courthouse hall, just outside the judge's chambers, while we quickly renewed our vows. By this point, the promised home in West Memphis on my mother's land was finished, so we began our whole new life there, even though we were planning to take off for New Mexico.

Before we set out for New Mexico, Jack got a job selling cars in Memphis at the Chevrolet dealership on Union Avenue. I worked at Berger Enterprises, my family business, in the office and wherever I was needed. For the fun of it, Jack decided one night that he wanted to be a waiter at Pancho's. A huge mistake. He was clumsy and spilled water on a customer. But Jack Jr. made one of his characteristic charming funny remarks, and the customer laughed.

At this point things were going well, and life seemed great. We went hunting and fishing together. Jack used Little Jack as a bird dog to run and retrieve the ducks. One day Jack took me fishing in the middle of nowhere in Arkansas. He had a boat hidden in a marsh. I have no idea how he'd arranged this; Andrew must have done it. Jack helped me into the boat, put in a cooler of drinks, and away we went.

After a while he asked me to hand him the cooler. I did and found that we had a big snake underneath. I sat the cooler back down and told Jack what I found. He picked up the paddle and knocked the snake into la la land and then put it into the water. I remember all of my experiences with Jack Jr. so vividly.

It was doomed to happen. Jack Jr. came home one morning around seven a.m. I asked where he had been. He said he was at the Shriners party. The Shriners that I knew were known for their wild parties with pretty women. I started crying, and he didn't want to deal with it. He was nonresponsive and nonchalant, as if nothing had happened. He seemed shocked to see me cry. I had so much hope for a better life and had put so much faith in Jack Jr. But I was hurt again. I felt as if I had been used. I felt like I was nothing. I also later figured out that I had postpartum syndrome after each child and each of my many miscarriages. I was depressed and a danger to myself.

When Jack went about his business as if nothing had happened, I felt trapped inside a body that I did not control. I knew what I was doing, and yet, I had no feelings. I went next door and found some of Mother's pills—valium, I think. I took a handful. Mother found me when I was still conscious and rushed me to Baptist Hospital in Memphis. They pumped my stomach. And then they put me in the psychiatric ward for observation for a few days. Jack Jr. never came to the hospital. Mother called Jack Goldsmith Sr., who made sure the episode did not make headlines in the newspapers.

A few days later, I was released and went home to West Memphis. My mother's heart and soul must have been about to burst with sadness and concern. But she kept her feelings inside and never discussed why I did what I did. She just took care of me. I eventually got back together with Jack Jr. I still believed what the Connecticut doctor told me, and I was still planning on having a new life in New Mexico.

At some point before Jack and I moved west, we took a brief trip to Las Vegas on a shuttle junket with my brother, his new wife, Sylvia, and a group of friends. Just before we departed for the airport, Jack offered me a marijuana cigarette. I didn't really want to try, but I did. I took a few drags, and I immediately felt silly.

When we arrived at the old Las Vegas airport several hours later, I was still woozy. After Jack and I descended the steps from the plane, I collapsed on the tarmac. Jack called an ambulance, and when I got to the hospital, I discovered that I had been pregnant but had had a miscarriage.

The doctors wanted me to spend the night in the hospital. Jack got me into a room and left for the hotel and casino, and I spent the night and most of the next day alone in the hospital and numb. I felt so alone. I didn't know how to get in touch with Jack, and I wasn't sure if or when he would show up. Jack appeared around four p.m. the next day, and when we arrived at the hotel, Mother was there to once again save the day. I was so happy to see her, since Jack was not very consoling about my miscarriage. We all spent the next few days gambling and having a pretty good time—Jack was very nice to me once I got to the hotel—and then returned to Memphis.

Jack and I finally moved west in November 1965. A huge moving truck packed our things, and we took off with Jack's two-seater MG, with Little Jack in the little space behind the seats where the convertible top went. Somewhere in Texas, we bought a tiny dog for Little Jack.

We also took a detour to Dallas, where Jack had spent time, since his mother was dating a man there. He stopped at a porn shop and bought a whole bunch of magazines. I probably should have thought this was an odd or offensive thing for him to do. Jack always had stacks of *Playboy* magazines in the bathroom cabinet wherever we lived. By this point, I was used to it, and it did not seem odd or offensive.

When we arrived in Santa Fe, we couldn't find a nice apartment that permitted both dogs and children. So, we continued on to Tucson, Arizona, after rerouting the moving van. We found a great new high-rise there with a grocery store and swimming pool.

After we settled in, Jack got a job selling cars and registered for the University of Arizona. I found a good Montessori School for Little Jack. He was just a little more than three years old and had the intelligence of an older boy. I signed up with the University of Chicago for a correspondence art class. I had to be with Little Jack when he got home from school. I did my homework in the morning or late at night. Things seemed to be going great.

Soon after we arrived, Jack's father visited and asked me to sign a contract reverting the ownership share of the high-rise to him so he could sell the building. He did not offer me money or anything else in return. I cannot explain why I signed it, but I did. Jack Sr. took advantage of me, and I never forgot that.

Unfortunately, it wasn't long before I suspected that Jack was screwing around again. One morning when I was cleaning the apartment, I found two drive-in movie ticket stubs on top of our dresser. I confronted Jack with my suspicion that he had taken someone else to the movies. As usual in these circumstances, he denied it and clammed up.

At about this time, around March of 1966, I discovered I was pregnant with my second child. I decided to return home, and Jack agreed to go back with me. I knew I did not want to be in Arizona with a new baby on the way and Jack starting or continuing to mess around. If my mother were writing this book, she would say, "You would think it would fall off after so many women."

Chapter 11

Brett, Steven,
and a Second Divorce

I was at home with Mother in West Memphis when my water broke.
Jack was not there. He was playing cards with my brother and his
friends, which he often did; he often lost lots of money. Mother took
me to the hospital and on September 16, 1966, I gave birth to my
second son, Brett Berger Goldsmith. He was a beautiful baby who
weighed eight pounds seven ounces. He was much mellower than his
brother, Little Jack, had been at birth.

We named Brett after the lead in the TV series *Maverick*. His
middle name, Berger, was my father's surname. I brought Brett home
and introduced him to his room in West Memphis I had decorated
in yellow.

After a couple of weeks, I took Brett for a checkup. I showed Dr.
Parker a place on Brett's bottom, like a pimple, that was not healing. It
turned out that Brett had a staph infection he contracted in the hospital
when he was born. We took him to the Catholic hospital where there was
a great surgeon for this problem. Jack showed up during the operation,
so I was not alone. The operation was successful, and Brett was fine.

When Brett was still a tiny baby and Little Jack was five, Jack Jr. and I, the boys, Mother, and Bertha took a trip to Miami Beach and stayed at the Americana Hotel. While there, Jack asked me to have some professional nude photographs taken. It was hard for me to do this. It was hard to give of myself to my husband who wanted naked pictures of me and who did not appreciate me just the way I was. But as usual, I agreed.

I arranged the shoot with the head photographer at the hotel, whom Jack had previously introduced me to. The photographer drove me from the hotel to a nearby nudist colony. We entered a wooded area and drove to an opening that had lounge chairs and one man sunbathing in the nude. I was extremely happy I did not have a huge audience.

I emerged from the changing area wrapped only in a towel. The photographer directed me into a swampy area where I waded into a couple feet of water and grabbed a palm tree. After he took a few shots I noticed a snake near my ankles. I immediately told the photographer to stop shooting. We went to a different area on dry land.

The photographer developed more than 100 photos the next day. He was a pro and took nice photos that were not risqué. I was happy with them and not ashamed. I showed them to Mother. She went through every one of them but never said a word about them. When Jack saw them, I could tell from his expression that he was shocked but very pleased.

I would have loved for him to say something—"you are beautiful," "thank you," anything. But it was like he had lockjaw. He didn't say a word. And he never looked at them again. It was like he'd gotten what he wanted, and that was that. I kept the photos in a lockbox and destroyed all but one, the one below, years later.

A picture from my photo shoot

When we got back to Memphis, Jack had a new idea for us to make money. He proposed to take out a life insurance policy on his life and leave it to me. Then he would go to South America and disappear, and I would collect the money and then join him there. They would never find us, and we would be set for life. I told him this was a terrible idea and would be illegal. He talked a little longer, trying to convince me that all would be fine and that we would be set for life. But I said, "No."

Jack decided he wanted a car dealership and found one for sale in Union City, Tennessee, 110 miles north of Memphis. Jack's father gave him the money and the loan support to get the dealership.

We bought a two-bedroom house on a paved country road with a huge yard surrounded by cornfields. Jack and Brett lived in the garage we'd converted to a bedroom. Mother once said she knew how to get to our Union City house because she could smell her way there.

On the road from Route 51 to our house were several fast-food drive-ins, the famous Reelfoot Meat Packing Plant, a town restaurant, and finally, Kentucky Fried Chicken on the corner of the country road we lived on, alongside corn, soybeans, and swine.

At Jack's suggestion, I shopped at Goldsmith's to furnish the new house. I especially loved our den, which looked out over the back yard with a swing set and toys. For Little Jack's seventh birthday, we got him a mini-Model T that he and Brett drove around the yard.

I loved our home and our life, at least briefly. I learned archery, croquet, horseshoes—all the fun games. I found a good helper; she was not Bertha, but she was good at cooking and taking care of the house. Jack and Brett played all day in the cornfields and often brought home several husks to have for dinner. There is nothing like really fresh corn on the cob. Corn off the cob was even better.

Once, when Mother was visiting, we were sitting in the den, while the boys were playing outside. All of a sudden, I heard her say, "Oh, my God, Brett's in trouble." She opened the door and ran out with me following her. Brett got his neck caught in the side bar of the swing set and was just hanging by his neck. I have trouble even mentioning this episode. Thank God for my mother. We eased him out, and he was shaken up but OK.

Another time, Brett found a large nail and somehow stuck it into a live electric socket outside. He came in crying and showed me what he had done. He'd gotten a good shock but was all right, thank goodness. Boys and their accidents can be quite a challenge.

My third son, Steven, was born in Union City on October 6, 1969. Only Mother was with me at the hospital. Unlike the births of my other two sons, I had Steven without being put to sleep because my blood pressure was bottoming out. So, this was the first time I felt my baby being born. It was very painful but worth it. We chose the name "Steven" after Jack's friend Steve Siddles, Jack's best friend. His middle name was "Carter," which was Geneva's maiden name. Steven was a beautiful and really good baby. He did not cry a lot and always seemed content. Mother and Bertha stayed for a few weeks to help me with Steven and the other boys.

I didn't know it, but my time with Jack was quickly running out. He was smoking a lot of marijuana that he kept hidden in a field near the car dealership. Soon after Steven was born, he started talking about couples he wanted us to be with. He mentioned a couple in New Orleans and kept pushing me to go there. I declined, and he dropped the conversation.

The new baby, the new business, and Mother being with me gave Jack the freedom to mess around as he wished. At some point, someone told me he was running a whorehouse. And then his business fell apart. Jack's father discovered that Jack had fraudulently used his name to get a second loan for his business. Jack also left his friend from Memphis, a business partner, high and dry.

I honestly do not know the last time I saw Jack. It was sometime in March 1970. One day I woke up, and he was just gone. I have no memory of even saying goodbye. (I would later learn that Jack left me to be with another woman who was pregnant with his child, who would be born six months after Steven). I was distraught and totally worn down by Jack Jr. I had been up and down like a yo-yo and was again all alone, this time with three boys. I called Mother and told her I was coming home with the boys, putting the house up for sale, and getting a lawyer for a divorce. I never wanted to see or hear from Jack Jr. again.

On July 6, 1970, I filed a Bill for Divorce from Jack Jr. Here is an excerpt:

> *Your Complainant would . . . show that the Defendant has always been a spend-thrift, spending large sums of money for his own use, benefit and pleasure, having no regard for the welfare of your Complainant and the minor children.*
>
> *Your Complainant has begged and pleaded with her husband to refrain from this misconduct and be a good father and husband, to no avail.*
>
> *Your Complainant would show that the Defendant has refused and neglected to assume the responsibilities of a husband and father and has acted as a single person.*
>
> *Your Complainant would further show that the Defendant employed the services of two females and organized a house of ill repute in Union City, Tennessee, which caused your Complainant much embarrassment and humiliation, not only for herself but for the three minor children.*
>
> *Your Complainant would further show that the Defendant constantly squandered money for his own personal pleasure; that*

he has gone to Las Vegas and gambled large sums of money and has run up heavy gambling debts.

Your Complainant would further show that the Defendant has been seen in the company of several women during the marriage, one of which . . . is one of the two females employed by the Defendant in his house of ill repute in Union City, Tennessee.

Your Complainant has begged and pleaded with her husband to refrain from this misconduct, stop humiliating her and the children, but to no avail, as he has continued in his open and notorious conduct.

While the divorce proceedings were pending, I felt I needed to get out of town to be alone. I was suffering from postpartum depression, and I was having out-of-body experiences. This is hard to explain. I was walking through life, but everything seemed strange. I was like a zombie. I was detached from my feelings. It was as if I were looking from outside in on my feelings, but I could not control them. And when I looked at things around me, the reality of the world did not register. I wanted to run away from these horrible emotions. It was a constant fight every day, and I decided I needed time for Brenda. So, I left the boys with Mother and Bertha and went to Acapulco, Mexico.

My hotel in Acapulco was small and did not have locks on the door. But I didn't care; I was not afraid. The morning after I arrived, I went to the patio for breakfast, and next to my table were two really good-looking young men. They were from Detroit. One of them, named Pat, looked like James Garner. He was really nice-looking. The men were about to go fishing and asked if I wanted to join. I did, and I had a great time. The next day, the three of us played golf; I remember iguanas all over the golf course. Pat asked if he could come to Memphis to visit me. I told him I was getting a divorce and had three boys. He was OK with that.

Back in Memphis, the divorce proceedings took place. I brought two of the prostitutes Jack employed from Union City as witnesses. Jack had skipped town and his whereabouts were unknown, so the divorce was uncontested.

On September 2, 1970, I got my second divorce from Jack Jr. The Court declared that Jack Jr. was a "fugitive from justice" who was "attempting to secret himself from the jurisdiction of this Court." The court also determined my "allegations in the original Bill for Divorce are true," and that Jack Jr. "is guilty of abandoning [me] and turning [me] out-of-doors and refusing and neglecting to support and provide for [me]." The judge awarded me custody of the boys, $300 per month in child support payments out of Jack Jr.'s trust fund, and Jack's stock rights in a company that didn't amount to much money. The Court also ruled that I was entitled to additional alimony and child support from Jack Jr. "whenever personal service of process can be obtained on this fugitive." More than fifty years later, I still have not received a penny from him.

In my experience, everything related to marriage—from virginity to divorce—is over in the blink of an eye.

Chapter 12

Bob Rivet

After the divorce, I was a single mother with three boys, no income, and no job. I told Mother I wanted to go back to work at Pancho's. She gave me a job in accounting in the office, which was then in West Memphis. The main thing I remember from this time was that my brother Louis Jack, who was running the company, often had his cronies come to his office to play cards.

My brother had moved into my house, next to Mother's, where Jack and I used to live. I had to live with Mother, which was comfortable. I slept with Mother in the king-size bed in her room, Steven had his own room, and Jack and Brett shared a room.

I remained depressed during this period. One day I went next door to talk to my brother. He was in bed with his wife. After some small talk, I blurted out that I was depressed but was doing better since I was talking to God. Instead of being supportive, he told me that God could not take away my depression, and that I had to do that myself. I told him that I trusted that God would be by my side, and then I walked away.

The next phase of my life was a continuation of swinging doors of men, one out and another in. My life moved like an airplane taking off, with someone else—not me—at the throttle.

For example, I visited the handsome man I met in Mexico, Pat, at his home in Detroit for a few days. I met his family, and we had a pretty good time. I remember visiting the Ford museum with him. The following week he visited me in West Memphis. We had dinner, and he slept on the couch at Mother's.

Early the next morning, while I was just waking up, I opened my eyes, and Pat was on his knees. He apologized for waking me but said he had to tell me something. "I love you; I love your boys, and I want to marry you, please," he said. I felt really bad, but as sweet, kind, and good-looking as he was, I was not interested in living in Detroit.

I met another man from Detroit just after I divorced Jack. His name was Charles O'Brien. He was a Teamsters Union official and he was very close to Jimmy Hoffa, the famous former Teamsters president.

I met Chuck through his mother, Sylvia Pagano, who became friends with my mother when they met at a motel pool in North Miami Beach in the early 1960s. She would always say nice things about her son when she visited Mother in West Memphis. I met Chuck briefly in the 1960s, when he would come to pick up Mother and accompany her to visit Sylvia in Detroit. We spent some time together, and one night, we even kissed. Chuck was handsome, but I was not too drawn to him then. He was going through a divorce and was preoccupied with his work. I liked him very much and trusted him, kind of like I trusted Billy, but we did not, at the time, have a serious relationship.

And then, a few days after the last time I saw Chuck, "ring, ring,"—the phone brought another man. It was a neurosurgeon from Lafayette, Louisiana, named Bob Rivet. I later learned that Bob earned his undergraduate and medical degrees from Louisiana State University and served as a paratrooper with the 101st Airborne (Screaming Eagles). My Tri Delta sister, Toni Wiley, knew Bob and urged him to call me. We started talking, but, almost immediately, I heard Brett crying. He told me he would call me back. I rushed to help Brett, who had fallen and hurt himself. He was OK after some hugs and loving.

Soon the phone rang again. After asking if Brett was OK, Bob asked if I had ever been to the Kentucky Derby, which was a week

Chuck O'Brien, about the time we first met

away. I had not. So, Bob invited me. His head nurse sent me airline tickets, instructed me where to meet him, and told me the schedule for the two days. It was very organized. It reminded me of Jack Jr., who had everyone do things for him.

I flew to Louisville, and Bob's uncle met me at the gate. He took me to the airport bar, where Bob was sitting alone with a drink and a package on the table. After introductions, we sat down. Bob handed me the package and said, "Welcome to the Kentucky Derby." I was usually skeptical of gifts from men. This gift was a beautiful gold watch with inlaid diamonds. A bit overboard, but fabulous. It made me nervous, though, as if I had to do a favor in return. I remembered Jack Jr. coming home with sexy underwear when he wanted something. I told Bob I could not accept it, and he got angry. He insisted and made a point that, when he did something, it was with meaning.

I accepted the beautiful watch and put it on. I was in a whole new world. My boys were safe, and I was hoping to have a good time. We talked for a while and then drove to the hotel. I checked in, and Bob showed me where to meet for the Churchill Downs get-together on the mezzanine. I showed up in a pretty dress. But crowds bothered me, and I didn't know anyone. I stood like a mummy. Small talk is not my thing.

In the middle of the event, Bob got an emergency call. A boy who had been shot with an arrow through his head, and on whom Bob had operated, had taken a turn for the worse. Bob had to take the next flight to Lafayette, and he asked me to join him. I did. We arrived, and he dropped me off at his home on the outskirts of Lafayette. It was a beautiful two-bedroom house, very warm and manly. It had a pool table and indoor swimming pool.

I was tired and went to bed. Bob came home early in the morning. He did not seem as tired as I was, so we sat on the sofa and talked.

Immediately, he asked me to marry him. Here I was again, in a get-married situation. I rambled on about how I couldn't because it was too quick, and I did not know him at all. Before he got quiet, he said he would take care of the boys and love them. Every man who asked to marry me after I divorced Jack always said they would take care of my boys, as if I were the fourth wheel.

The last night, Bob threw a huge party with all of his friends. He loved having people around him. But in my continuing postpartum depression, I felt suffocated by all the people around and went to his bedroom. My friend Toni found me and tried to get me to join the party. But I could not. Bob asked what was wrong, and I told him I did not like crowds. He put his arms around me and lifted me up and held me as if to protect me.

The next day Bob took me to his office. This was a couple of hours before my plane was due to leave. Again, I felt overwhelmed. I was at a hospital in a place I did not know with a neurosurgeon I barely knew, who had asked me to marry him within hours after meeting me. It was too much for me to handle.

A few weeks after I returned home, Bob flew to the West Memphis airport on a private plane for about 24 hours. I picked Bob up and took him to Mother's house. Aunt Florene was there. We hung out and talked. Before dinner time, Bob and I went grocery shopping, and he cooked a Cajun dinner. Mother was not impressed and not happy with him at all. My Aunt Florene did not like him, either. They didn't like him because he was being so pushy about getting married. Bob left early the next morning.

Bob continued to court me. He loved music and sent me records that I played over and over. It drove my mother and the boys crazy when I played these records every day. "I Love You More Today

Than Yesterday," by Stevie Wonder, was my favorite. While in West Memphis, I made Bob a scrapbook of the LSU football team, a team he loved (and for which he would one day become the head doctor).

I eventually agreed to marry Bob. I wanted someone who could take care of my boys, which Bob promised to do. I shipped our personal items to Lafayette, rented a Volkswagen bug, stuffed the three boys in it, and drove to Lafayette. We married on Christmas Day at Bob's house. I wore a beautiful canary-yellow dress that looked like something Elizabeth Taylor would wear. The boys were there, and I was pretty calm.

Bertha took care of the boys in Lafayette while we honeymooned in Puerto Rico. We stopped off in New Orleans to meet his mother, sister, and uncle. His mother was not very nice to me. Bob asked her, a seamstress, to shorten the navy-and-white dress I was wearing. Oh, boy—another husband who wants to change me. Jack wanted me to dress in sexy lingerie. Bob wanted my dresses short even though the style was to wear them longer. At least one good thing happened on our stopover in New Orleans: I got a delicious Cajun gumbo recipe from Bob's sister that I have to this day. I liked her; she was sweet to me.

We made it to Puerto Rico and had a wonderful room with a balcony overlooking the ocean. We had fun and enjoyed the ocean. The San Juan beach was breathtaking, and the water was azure blue. We returned to Lafayette, and the boys were fine, but Bertha was not so fine. "Miss Brenda, I have to get home!" she told me when we arrived. She did not like Cajun country or Bob's cook, who was into voodoo. I immediately arranged for Bertha to return to West Memphis. Bless her heart—she was in tears.

Then it became time for me to face reality and get used to Cajun life. Cajun life was full of fun, laughter, and booze. Bob loved Cajun food and had a great Southern Cajun cook. He also loved horses. We went to the track, Evangeline Downs, about once every two weeks. Bob bought a Quarter Horse that he named "Brenda's Gal." She was a decent horse and won a couple of races. I remember a nice photo of the two of us with a blanket of flowers across Brenda's Gal.

I liked the horses. I also got involved with charities, including fashion shows to raise money and luncheons to organize fundraising events. As life went on this became a passion of mine—helping people. I got this from my mother and always made a space in my life to do for others, regardless of what was going on in my life.

Bob liked to have a couple of huge parties every month. I hated them. Our home was filled with people who loved to eat and drink. Bob drank vodka and grapefruit juice. It would drive me crazy when he swirled his drink and ice with his index finger. The problem at these parties was that the drinks came early, and the food came late. Not good. Many conversations at the parties were about politics. I paid zero attention. Bob would pass out at the end of each party, except when an emergency came up at the hospital during the party. When that happened, Bob would inhale oxygen from a tank in his closet to sober up.

Bob was definitely the Big Man in the room during these parties. Everyone praised him: the great and talented Dr. Rivet. Bob flirted incessantly with women. I often wondered if I selected men on the prowl or if all men were that way. I suppose all men are not that way, at least I pray not. I started to think I should have known Bob better before I married him. That would have been a good idea. *Just use your head, Brenda, for a little longer, before saying, "Yes."*

One day a few months after I moved to Lafayette, my friend Toni, who had introduced me to Bob, visited me at home. I did not feel well. She suggested I get a pregnancy test, and sure enough, I was pregnant. I was shocked. I had a cyst taken off my ovary just before Bob and I got married, and I didn't think I could get pregnant again. I was really upset. I didn't want to have another child. I cannot explain why, but it just seemed not to fit with my life with Bob. I loved my three boys; they were perfect, and I did not want another child to interfere with our relationship.

I woke up the next morning very, very depressed, like I was at the bottom of a pit. Mother called that morning, and I had a very negative reaction. I worried that she would ask if I was OK, or how things were going with Bob, or how the boys were. I didn't want to hear it or to have a conversation; I didn't want to have to explain anything. I hung up the phone.

I then grabbed all the medicine Bob had around the house and got in my car. (Jack and Brett were already in school, and Steven was with the babysitter). I drove to a motel, checked in, went straight to my room, emptied a big pile of pills into my hand, shoved them in my mouth, swallowed them with a glass of water, and immediately felt like my world was ending.

I remember being semi-passed out on the floor. I crawled to the phone, lifted the receiver, dialed zero, and told the hotel operator that I didn't want to die. The next thing I knew, I was waking up in a hospital, and a gynecologist told me I'd had a tubal pregnancy, had been operated on, and that I was going to be all right.

Bob had me admitted to a psychiatric ward for observation. I remember one day resting in bed when a lady walked into my room. I asked her if I could help. She said she was looking for something. Her purse, she said. She was feeling the walls with her hands, up and down, in my room and in the bathroom. Finally, she gave up and left without a word. Life in a psychiatric ward, I guess.

Bob never came to see me. I was not allowed to have visitors. Bob did come by and talk to the nurses. He had a wonderful side of him, thank goodness. I kept asking the nurse to please find out how my sons were. She told me that they were fine. I later learned that Mother sent Bertha to take care of the boys. For reasons I never understood, Mother never came to Lafayette while I was in the hospital.

I stayed in the hospital for about a week and then went home. I was thrilled to be out of that place and free. When I got home, Bob gave me a hug, but we never talked about what happened. The doctors told him to act like everything was normal.

Mother visited about a week later. She was with Lou Dalitz, the brother of the famous Las Vegas gangster Moe Dalitz. She had met Lou through Sylvia Pagano, Chuck O'Brien's mother. Bob was excited to meet Lou because of his connections to gambling and the mob. Mother and Lou stayed in one of the upstairs bedrooms. Mother and I never talked about my attempted suicide; she never asked me about it, and I didn't want to discuss it anyway. Mother spent most of the trip out on the roof sunbathing. Bob and Lou had fun together talking and drinking.

Pretty soon, my life seemed to return to normal. For some reason, I wasn't as depressed anymore, at least for a while. I cut my hair very short—about two inches all around. That was my postpartum depression personality. I am surprised I did not shave my head.

Once I got out of the institution, I enjoyed the boys so much. In one football game, Brett intercepted a pass and ran it down the field to the wrong end zone, figured out his mistake, and ran the whole length of the field to score an actual touchdown. He was so adorable running about, while the other team was trying to tackle him.

One day Bob took me for a drive to show me some land that he loved, located on a bayou tributary of the Vermillion River. Bob said we could build a dream home, and he did not set a budget. I started getting busy designing a fabulous home. I visualized a Southern mansion like in "Gone with the Wind." I, of course, asked Bob what he liked and wanted in the house.

I enjoyed Bob's happy personality when he was sober, and we loved playing billiards at home on his pool table. We also played bridge with Debbie and Jerry Young, our closest friends—that was fun. My crazy project was dying the carpet in the room where the pool table was. It was a light color and had spots all over. I dyed it black. It worked out so-so, but it looked better than before.

Bob became more demanding and yelled more and more as time went on—especially when he was drinking. Bob would start with his vodka and grapefruit juice as soon as he arrived home, around six in the evening, before dinner. He yelled at me once because he thought I was too nice to a photographer who took pictures of me and the boys.

Another time he yelled at me because I was spending too much time with the boys' football and baseball coach, organizing the boys' sports events. There was nothing at all going on, of course, but Bob still didn't like it. This was all very distressing. It reminded me of my father accusing my mother of flirting and being with men. I especially did not like the yelling, because the boys could hear it.

At about this time, I got a call from Jack Jr. I think Mother had arranged it. Jack asked me to meet him in Santa Monica, California. I told Bob I was taking the boys to visit Mother in Ft. Lauderdale. But after I dropped the boys off with Mother at the Bahia Mar, I flew to Santa Monica to see Jack. I planned to be there two nights. I packed a photo of myself and the boys to give to him.

I arrived at the hotel in Santa Monica around an hour before Jack arrived. He came to my room carrying a large Louis Vuitton suitcase.

"That is the ugliest thing I have ever seen," I blurted out. I was still in a bad and rather hateful mood because he had left me and the boys high and dry. I was there because I was hoping he had changed. Jack raised his eyebrows and looked at me with his beautiful eyes, as if to say, "Where did *that* come from?" He immediately asked to have sex. No mention of the boys. I showed him the picture I brought, which I had placed on the windowsill. He looked at it, but that was it—he did not ask about the boys at all. Despite Jack's indifference to his children, I agreed to have sex with him.

Jack quickly left—he was always in a hurry. That evening he picked me up and took me to a lovely restaurant on Sunset Boulevard. It was near the Whiskey a Go Go, the nightclub where Johnny Rivers recorded his famous version of "Hello, Operator, Give Me Memphis, Tennessee."

Halfway through the meal, Jack asked me if I wanted to work the crossword puzzle on the dance floor after dinner. There was a spotlight shining on the table that had a crossword puzzle and chairs around the table. I did not realize it, but the deal was that whoever sat at the puzzle table was signaling that they wanted to have sex with another couple. A nice-looking couple approached and asked if we were married. Jack told them we were divorced.

They then asked if we were interested in going home with them. Jack said "Yes," but added, "the reason I divorced her is that she is going to say 'No.'" The couple immediately left. Jack was not happy, but I was even less happy. My plane was due to take off the next evening, but I changed it to an afternoon flight.

The next morning Jack picked me up. He had asked me to wear a bathing suit. We took a short drive north up the Pacific Coast Highway, parked, and walked down an incline onto the beach area. Jack asked me to undress. We were at a nude beach. I became furious, got dressed, and made him take me to the airport right away after stopping by the hotel to pick up my luggage. We went inside the airport and sat in a diner waiting for my plane. Jack looked at me like a lost puppy, and said to me, in a very serious voice: "If I ever, ever ask you to come see me again, do not come." I told him he had nothing to worry about. Time took care of my disgust for him, as it hurt too much to carry around hate.

Back in Louisiana, my depression was growing worse. Bob suggested that reverse hypnosis might help. I agreed and went to see a doctor, who put me in a relaxing state and hypnotized me by having me count backwards and other techniques. At some point in the therapy, I began to cry. The doctor asked what I was crying about. I told him it was because my father was not with us. "Why is he not with you?" asked the doctor. "He does not love me," I said. "Why not?" asked the doctor. "Mother said he does not love us," I said. This, I think, was at the heart of my depression all these years.

The end in Louisiana came soon. One day I came home to the last house where we lived in Lafayette—a rural place with a huge tree near the driveway. The boys were high in the tree, in a tree house they had built. They were painting it white, and the white paint was all over them. I panicked. Can you imagine being half out of your mind with untreated postpartum depression, and you see your three young children dangling from tree limbs covered in white paint head to toe? After about three hours and two or three baths and showers, I had them looking as if they belonged to me again.

This event set me off. I was exhausted, and I could not give of myself to anyone. I told Bob that evening that I wanted to leave him. A few days later, I departed Lafayette with my boys.

Chapter 13

Chuck O'Brien

I put the boys in my station wagon and drove to Florida. My father was living in Plantation, near Ft. Lauderdale. He was wonderful in helping me find a new two-bedroom apartment near him. It was across the street from Jacaranda Golf Course and had a canal nearby. There were also fields nearby with cows, where high school children would gather mushrooms and get high.

The boys had plenty of places to fish and throw the football. Jack caught snakes, with Brett as his assistant, pounding them with a stick or shooting them with his BB gun. Then he skinned the snakes. Brett was the fisherman. He and Daddy fished in the canals near our apartment. My father called Brett his "Little Partner." He called Steven "Little Einstein."

Mother arrived and helped me buy furniture. I purchased bunk beds to try to make the boys feel comfortable and not so crowded. She didn't let me buy from one furniture company because it was run by the mafia, which enforced non-payments with painful penalties. How my small-town mother knew so much was beyond me.

Once I got the boys settled, Bob started calling. He missed me and wanted to come to Florida to see me. Before I knew it, he was in my bedroom, and we were on our way to sleep. I had a horrible nightmare: I was sleeping with the devil. When I woke up, I actually saw the devil lying next to me. That was a blinking red light. Bob left the next day, and I quickly got a divorce in Florida.

This was a low point in my life. I had just gotten out of a mental hospital and divorced my second husband, and my life seemed perpetually on the run. Most importantly, I knew I needed help in taking care of my three young boys. I didn't know what to do, so I reached out to the one man whom I thought was a friend, whom I trusted, and who might help: Chuck O'Brien.

I knew Chuck worked for a labor union in Detroit. I called the AFL-CIO Local. He did not work there—he was in the Teamsters Union—but amazingly, the AFL-CIO receptionist knew Chuck and gave me his number. I then called Teamsters Local 299 in Detroit and left a message for Chuck. Within a few hours, he returned my call. I told him I needed help and that my boys did, too. I said that we were leaving Florida to stay with Mother in West Memphis in the next few days. "I am coming," he told me.

When Chuck arrived one evening in West Memphis, I was elated and felt safe. Soon Chuck met my father. We were at Mother's house, in the den. Chuck greeted Daddy and would not stop talking. Daddy was interested in Chuck and his stories. He was totally different from the other men I had relationships with.

Chuck and I spent time with the boys, and he kept talking about how much his mother loved Little Jack. After the boys went to bed, Chuck and I sat and talked in the living room. At this point I had no interest in another relationship, much less another marriage. I asked Chuck a lot of questions related to finances, and especially about how I might make money off of property I owned near Pancho's—perhaps as a truck stop, which he knew a lot about. Somehow or another Chuck and I ended up on the floor in front of the fireplace, with Chuck holding me. That night he asked if the boys and I would come to Detroit, where he lived, and stay with him at the home of his friends, Marvin and Betty Adell.

In the next five weeks or so, before we visited Detroit, Chuck and I spoke a lot on the phone. Chuck liked to talk. He asked me over and over about the boys. He had been divorced for a few years, and he told me about his hopes and dreams. I was drawn to him for many reasons. He was a kind and decent person. When he visited West Memphis, he was good to the boys. He was outgoing—he liked meeting everyone.

And Chuck was funny. He made me laugh. He also revealed his troubles to me. He was broke and in debt, primarily, he said, because of his divorce. He owed the IRS money and did not have a home of his own. That is why he was living with his friends the Adells in Detroit. Chuck told me he would be able to overcome these issues, and I did not worry about them.

The boys and I went to Detroit to see Chuck and the Adells in January 1975. The boys enjoyed sledding on a snow-covered hill, and we watched Chuck's son Chuckie play hockey for Hillsdale College. All five of us slept in a small bedroom together. One night, when the boys were asleep, Chuck asked me to marry him.

Again, a quickie proposal. And again, I agreed. My brain was churning, but I had to face the outside world. I know this was fast, but I felt like I knew and trusted Chuck better than prior husbands because I had known his mother, who had been friends with my mother. I was still distraught from all that I had been through, but, with Chuck, I felt safer. He was a good man.

When Chuck asked me to marry him, he was in a very difficult relationship with Jimmy Hoffa. Chuck had been very close to Hoffa ever since he was a boy—many people thought he was Hoffa's son. He had been Hoffa's right-hand man through all of his adventures and troubles since the 1950s, including Hoffa's famous fights with Bobby Kennedy. Chuck visited Hoffa monthly when he was in prison and spent a lot of time with him after he was released, when Hoffa was trying to regain control of the Teamsters Union.

Chuck was very worried that Hoffa was saying things he should not have been saying. One evening, a show came on TV, and Mr. Hoffa was giving an interview. Chuck was shaking his head. "I told him not to do that show," Chuck said. "I told him it would be bad for him." Chuck did not go into detail, and I did not watch what it was all about. Chuck just blurted out he is talking about the "outfit"—Chuck's word for the mafia—and he should not do that.

I sensed then that Chuck's relationship was strained. I did not know it at the time, but I had caused Chuck and Hoffa to have a falling-out. I told Chuck I did not want to live in Detroit. I wanted to go back to Florida so my boys could stay together in boarding school. Chuck told Hoffa that he was moving to Florida to be with his new family. Hoffa was furious, because Chuck had always been by his side. I had become a huge wedge between Chuck and Mr. Hoffa. The same story was going on in my home. Mother was telling me I was making a mistake.

One morning in West Memphis, a few months after Chuck and I were engaged, the phone rang, and I answered it; it was Hoffa. "This is Jimmy Hoffa. I want to speak with Chuckie," he said. I gave the phone to Chuck.

Chuck listened and then said, "I am happy, I have a new life, and I want to be with Brenda." Hoffa told him he would be fired on the spot as soon as he showed up for his new job with the Southern Conference of Teamsters, in Hallandale, Florida. Chuck stood his ground, and that was the end of the conversation. I felt bad, as I did not really understand the full story, and Chuck did not really go into detail.

On the day of our wedding, June 16, 1975, Chuck wanted the boys to be with us. So, we all piled into the car in West Memphis and went across the river to find someone to marry us. I don't remember what I was wearing, but it wasn't the wedding dress I had cherished since I was a girl. That dress was still in my scrapbook and not on my body. That is where it will always remain.

We stopped by three churches. I wanted to get married in the Unitarian church on the Mississippi River, but it was closed. Two other churches were closed, and one was Catholic and would not marry us. Chuck was getting nervous that we could not find anyone to marry us. He then got the idea to go to the courthouse. All five of us entered the cement halls of the Shelby County Courthouse on Adams Avenue in Memphis.

Brett, who was eight years old at the time, blurted out to the first person we passed, "Can you marry us?" It turned out that the man was Judge Otis Higgs. He said that he could marry us and gave us instructions on how to get to his chambers. Thirty minutes later, Chuck and I were married. We used vows from a wooden plaque with an Indian marriage ceremony that he had picked up at the Memphis airport and given me a month earlier. He wrote on the plaque: "Dedicated to Brenda Lou. Love always, Chuck."

Now we had to face Mother. The door at her house was locked. When she opened the door, we all saw that she had painted her face like a sad clown. She had huge lips, and even larger tears painted coming from her eyes. Mother had ruined a happy day. Mother was almost always wonderful to me throughout my life, but every time I tried to separate from her, she became a different person. She was always a good actress—like when she would stage a heart attack when Daddy would threaten her.

That night we celebrated our honeymoon in the Hilton Inn at the Memphis airport. Next door to us, there was a big party with people smoking marijuana. The smell was overwhelming. We got in bed right away, and Chuck was not in a good mood. The smell had him not high, but very low—or possibly high in a way he had never been before. Chuck was not a smoker or a drinker, so he was not happy. He was so into himself and his temper that sex did not even enter his mind. I put my head on his high chest and within a very few minutes he was knocked out. We returned home early the next morning, as Chuck was an early riser.

A few weeks later, we decided we wanted special wedding rings. I went to a jeweler in Memphis and told them we wanted a great designer. They recommended a woman in Kansas. I told her I wanted a ring that represented love. (It might seem strange, but my ability to design my ring was a form of freedom that other husbands did not give me; Chuck was always very supportive of my independence).

She delivered a beautiful design. It had a fish coupled with the cross to express the freedom of the spirit. She used the Greek symbols for alpha and omega to symbolize return. It had a symbol that represented *amare*, the Latin word for "love." The ring itself symbolized infinity. It had a chalice as a symbol of faith. And it had the inscription: "Then you will know the truth, and the truth will set you free," from John 8:32.

Chapter 14

Jimmy Hoffa
Disappears

Our first few weeks of marriage were great. We were all about to leave for Florida. In late July, Chuck had to return to Detroit to pack up the things in his office, and he left his black Lincoln Continental with us in West Memphis. While he was there, the boys, Mother, Bertha, and I took a trip to Hot Springs in Chuck's car. We got a motel room at the Holiday Inn and the next day arranged for a fishing trip with the boys. On the afternoon of July 31, we returned to the motel from fishing. When we walked into the hotel room, Mother was there. I could tell that something was wrong. She was calm but to the point.

"The news is saying that Hoffa is missing," Mother told me. Jimmy Hoffa's famous disappearance had occurred the day before, when he was last seen in the afternoon outside the Machus Red Fox restaurant in suburban Detroit. The disappearance had become news the next day.

Mother told me that she called Anthony Giacalone, a businessman in Detroit, whom Chuck had known as long as he had known Hoffa. Mother had "Uncle Tony's" number because she had met him on her trips to Detroit when she visited Sylvia Pagano, Chuck's mother. "Tony said Chuck is fine. He is on the streets trying to figure out what happened to Mr. Hoffa." At this point, I was not worried. I did not understand the significance of what had happened. Soon Chuck called and told me he was trying to find out what happened to Hoffa. He was short and to the point.

A few days later, Chuck came back to West Memphis. He was worn out and kept saying that "we" were trying to find out what happened. That night Chuck was still upset, and he jammed a chair under the front doorknob to keep out intruders. He told me it was a trick that Uncle Tony taught him—one that would enable him to hear if someone was trying to break in. I was taken back to my lockdown days with Mother—prison time again.

The next day we were all watching the evening news, and to our astonishment, one of the top stories was that Chuck O'Brien, a close confidant of Hoffa's, was also missing. "You're not missing—you're here!" said Brett. It is hard to explain to your children that the man you just married, their new father, is a leading suspect in a disappearance. I hated to put them through what they were about to go through.

The next day, all hell broke loose. Hoffa's son accused Chuck of being involved in Hoffa's disappearance, and, from that point on, Chuck was a leading suspect on the front pages of all the newspapers. The papers all mentioned that Chuck's whereabouts on the day of the disappearance were unknown, and that he was close to the mob figures who were also suspects in Hoffa's disappearance. The news media descended on West Memphis, and it was a circus. Chuck directed them all to the backyard and spoke with them there.

The next day the FBI showed up. When the agent knocked on Mother's door, she said "Hi, Red. How have you been?" Chuck was always amazed that Mother knew FBI agents. The agents said they wanted to interview me, and she sent them next door. They asked me about my trip to Hot Springs. Why did I go there? Where did I stay? Why did I have Chuck's car? When was I fishing, and when did I return? Then they started in on Mr. Hoffa. Had I seen him there? Was he supposed to be there? Had Chuck been in Hot Springs?

Now I was in a situation I had no control over. I was nervous—I had never talked to the FBI before, but I answered all their questions. And then other things started happening. The story about Chuck and the disappearance in *The Commercial Appeal* talked about his recent marriage to me and had my high school picture.

The newspapers in Hot Springs said that FBI agents were dredging the lake where we had fished, looking for Hoffa's body. *TIME* magazine suggested that I caused Chuck's break with Hoffa. It said that he had recently married a "go-go girl" and "did not receive the full blessing of Hoffa, who has his puritanical side." I was never a go-go girl; they must have been thinking about the go-go girls who performed at the El Toro Lounge next to Pancho's.

In Early August, Chuck returned to Detroit to have an interview with FBI agents. The agents trailed him at the airport and on the airplane—something he was used to since the FBI had followed him starting in the late 1950s because of his relationship to Hoffa. The FBI interviewed Chuck at the Detroit airport when he arrived there. Chuck wanted to be interviewed there for his own safety. They asked him detailed questions about his relationship to Hoffa and what he had been doing before, during, and after the day of the disappearance.

After that interview, the headlines got worse and worse. They had discovered blood in the back of the car that he was driving the day of the disappearance. It was later proven to be fish blood—he had been delivering a leaking frozen salmon to the Detroit suburbs on the afternoon Hoffa disappeared. But even though it was fish blood, the FBI and Hoffa's son were pointing the finger at Chuck as the leading suspect. They also prominently accused Anthony Giacalone and Anthony Provenzano, two close friends of Chuck's whom the newspapers said were in the mob.

So, it was time to take off for Florida with the boys in Chuck's Lincoln Continental. Chuck was happy to have the three boys to play with, and guide, and tease. As we drove the three boys were in the back seat, playing a game of "beep, beep," counting the number of Volkswagen Beetles. Jack and Brett had an advantage over Steven, since they were taller. But Steven still managed to win the games sometimes.

Chuck stopped in Chattanooga, Tennessee, to see one of his closest friends, Brownie, a lawyer Chuck had known ever since Brownie represented Hoffa in the Chattanooga trial brought by Bobby Kennedy in the 1960s. Brownie had a daughter, Jamie, whom Brett fell for. She was blond and adorable. They hit it off immediately.

After we left Chattanooga, somewhere in Florida, Chuck turned the radio on to listen to the news. Soon a story came on that was all about Chuck, the fish, the blood in the car, and the suspicions about him. The news was filled with the Hoffa story and Chuck's role in it. I could not believe it was happening, and I could not take it. I asked Chuck to please turn off the news. He did not listen. I finally could not take any more and told him if he did not turn it off, I was going to jump out of the car. He still did not turn it off. I reached over myself and turned the dial off—finally, silence. The Hoffa story was traumatizing me. I had a meltdown and asked Chuck to pull over somewhere so I could get out of the car and walk for a while. He did, and I got out and walked until I felt a bit better. I got back into a car where you could hear a pin drop.

The next evening, we arrived at the Teamster-owned country club and golf course called Rolling Hills in Ft. Lauderdale. We stayed short-term at the lodge on the property. It was lovely and spacious for all of us. The boys seemed very happy to have the space and a new beginning. The golf carts were at their disposal. Soon after we arrived, Chuck was served with papers to repossess his Lincoln because he had not made the payments. Things like this would happen a lot—we had lots of financial problems at the outset of our marriage because of Chuck's debts. Chuck was a kidnapping or murder suspect, had a new family, a new job, no real home, no transportation, and no income (since the IRS was taking all of his money).

Chuck got in touch with his boss, Joe Morgan, the head of the Southern Conference of Teamsters, to get a car. Mr. Morgan told Chuck to go to the Lincoln Mercury dealership in Hollywood and select a Lincoln for his company car.

While we lived in Rolling Hills, I had another meltdown when I got a subpoena from the Hoffa Grand Jury in Detroit saying that I had to be in court on a particular date. That was all I needed. Again, I had been brought onto the firing range. In a very emotional state, I told Chuck that I was not going to Detroit and that he had better get it worked out.

He knew I meant what I said and immediately got a doctor's letter explaining my emotional state. The letter said that I suffered from "hysterical neurosis" and might suffer "an emotional collapse" if I had to testify. Chuck presented me with the letter in a serious way and with very few words. He seemed proud and very relieved. The Judge excused me, thank goodness. Chuck often took responsibilities that I was carrying off my shoulders.

Even though I escaped the Grand Jury, at this point, I was starting to get down. I had just married Chuck and hoped for a wonderful new life with him. And now he was suddenly the leading suspect in a famous crime, and I and the boys had been sucked into the whole mess. I started to think I would never, ever get my life straight.

We next moved to the Executive House at the Inverrary golf course in Lauderhill. While there, I met Charlie Pride, a famous country singer. Soon after we arrived, Chuck offered my assistance to design the waitresses' outfits. He never told me he was doing this—he just did it. He said that my assistance with design would be the payment on the rent for our rooms. I said that was ridiculous. This was my first experience of Chuck "back-dooring me"—he would offer my services for projects without asking me first.

Chuck backdoored me again when he invited Jamie from Chattanooga to visit us without telling me. Brett was excited, but I was shocked as I did not learn about it until Jamie showed up. This was when I realized how happy I was to have boys instead of girls. Jamie was sweet but had a mind of her own. We were all getting ready to go down to the restaurant to eat, and I had to help Jamie get dressed. She wanted a bow in her hair, on which she instructed me how to make it and where she wanted it placed on her head. This took 30 minutes of "No, no, no—that is not right." I kept telling myself, *Thank goodness God gave me boys.*

The next day we all went to Florida Air Academy, a military boarding school that Little Jack had attended for a year, to get all three boys registered. I put the boys in that school because I was not well. I wanted the boys together; I thought the discipline of the school would be good for them, and Little Jack liked it during his first year. Jamie was with us the day we registered. I was glad she was there, since Brett was not happy about going to boarding school, and Jamie made it easier to take.

Chuck and I would often visit the boys at FAA. We watched Jack's and Brett's sports events, and Steven's plays. We watched the boys' parades. Little Jack was involved in a car wash at FAA to raise money for his sports teams. Every Friday afternoon, Chuck would take his car to be washed, and Jack was so happy to see him.

Chuck with boys at Florida Air Academy

Once, when Chuck was out of town, Uncle Tony Giacalone and his wife Zina came to visit and check on the boys at FAA. The Giacalones lived in Miami beach during the winter. Steven, who was only six years old, asked the Giacalones to take him to a drugstore to buy a card for my birthday. At the drugstore, Steven picked out a card. At the register, Uncle Tony started to pay for the card. Steven spoke up and told him that he would like to pay for it. He said it wouldn't be a gift from him if he didn't. So, so sweet—my heart skipped a beat when I heard this.

During the week, when the boys were at FAA, I kept myself busy oil painting football scenes. One was the Baltimore Colts for Jack and the other was the Dallas Cowboys for Brett. The boys would come home from Florida Air Academy on the weekends. It made them happy to come home. On the weekends, Steven was mainly with me. We lived by a lake, and Brett and I would fish. Of course, we also had alligators for neighbors. You could see their eyeballs sticking out of the water, their whole body in the water, or sunning on the shore. I had to be very cautious with the boys around the lake.

Next, we moved to a small house on the golf course at Inverrary, three houses down from Jackie Gleason. All three of the boys were set up in the garage because the townhouse was a one-bedroom. Chuck began his new job at the Southern Conference of Teamsters. He represented workers in the movie industry, construction workers across the South, including at Disney World and the Tennessee Valley Authority, known as TVA. For decades, every aspect of Chuck's life had been about the workers and their livelihoods. He had a big heart for people.

My stress levels went through the roof during this period. Chuck was traveling a lot for his job. This is when I realized that Chuck would be a revolving door: Home one day and gone the next, arriving home late or early mornings. No matter when he came, it was a good feeling to see him come through the door. He was still the leading suspect in the Hoffa disappearance, and the news stories and the constant FBI surveillance continued. It was a never-ending nightmare. My body and mind were traumatized, and I was getting tired. I couldn't deal with the confusion inside of me. Everything was off-kilter in my brain. I was trying to cope and protect myself as much as possible. I knew I needed help.

I started to see Dr. James Jordan, a psychiatrist in Ft. Lauderdale. I told him about my life and what was bothering me. He first started treating me with tranquilizers. They didn't work. The clock kept ticking, and I felt like I was going further downhill. I told Dr. Jordan I did not see an end to my trauma. I had a lot of faith in Dr. Jordan's suggestions for my sanity. He made the decision that I should have shock treatments to end my stress. Chuck was totally against it, and, from that day, on Dr. Jordan was an enemy.

I was given the treatments at the Broward hospital in Ft. Lauderdale. Chuck later called it the "full jolt." They sedated me a little and then put a stick like a popsicle stick between my teeth to prevent me from swallowing my tongue. After that I was out of it, and the equipment next to me was connected with tubes and suction cups to different parts of my head. I remember the electrical shock for just a second. I don't remember anything more about that shock treatment or any of the dozen or so subsequent ones. Chuck told everyone it was the worst thing he had experienced or seen.

I vaguely remember that, in the hospital, I had a roommate who wanted to be a beauty queen. I just listened as best as I could. I also had lunch with a man my age who was very kind, but I do not remember our conversations or if he had shock treatments. We were both very quiet. It would hurt my head in a weird way to think about anything. This was before I was finished with the treatments.

The next thing I remember is Chuck driving me home down Broward Boulevard in Ft. Lauderdale. When I would try to remember a past event, my head would feel like it was full of air. I would have a sensation—a funny feeling of my brain expanding—but I also had the impulse to try not to remember. I told Chuck I could not discuss certain things because it hurt my head. He was respectful, and we just got quiet. Gradually, each day got better. The shock treatments had attacked my past and eliminated the junk in my mind. To this day, if I try to go back in time about unpleasant things, I have that same feeling of resistance and air in my head.

Chuck always told me how much he loved me, and he gave me lots of cards and books to express his love. He often wrote on them, "Always and forever, My Brenda Lou." Because of my illness throughout my life and feelings about men, I never felt that I was his Brenda Lou, and I never felt his love, even though, throughout our marriage, he gave it to me. When Chuck offered love, for some reason, I would reject it. Maybe it was because I was afraid of love because of my father, or past husbands, or because I was sexually abused, or because I'd been mistreated by my brother.

Chapter 15

Life with Chuck

Being around Chuck meant hearing a lot of curse words. Four-letter words were a core part of his vocabulary. These words were directed mainly at the FBI, which harassed him all his life; at Jimmy Hoffa, Jr., who accused him of being involved in his father's disappearance; and to the Kennedys, who hounded him and Hoffa for years.

Chuck loved my three boys, and soon after we got to Florida, he asked if he could adopt them. I thought about it and discussed it with the boys. They were excited. They adored Chuck, who was a great father to them, despite his troubles. So, Chuck became their father, and they changed their names to "O'Brien."

In June of 1977, my son Jack graduated from Florida Air Academy in ninth grade. He was the head cadet and had a chest full of medals—more than any cadet ever. That fall, all of the boys started at Pine Crest School in Ft. Lauderdale. Pine Crest was and remains an excellent private school. But it was expensive. I told Mother the boys needed to go there, and she agreed to pay for it. My brother went bonkers over that decision.

About six months after the boys started at Pine Crest, the principal's office received a call that the O'Brien boys were going to be kidnapped. The lower school principal called me at home. She told me about the call and said the boys were safe in her office. I collected the boys and took them home. They stayed home for several days. The school did not want them back, but Chuck convinced them. Chuck told me the FBI would watch them, but that did not sit well with me. Nonetheless, I returned the boys to school, even though I worried about it.

Chuck had his problems, but he was always a very good father to my three boys, and he was very protective. No one could say anything against them or try to hurt them. He protected them from everyone. The boys' friends liked Chuck, too. He would go to sports practices, and he was friends with the coaches.

Chuck also took care of some of the boarding students in the dorms. He would take them to dinner or a show with my boys, and made sure they were not homesick. I think the reason Chuck was so good at taking care of young people was that he was lonely and somewhat neglected as a child. His mother was single and busy working, and would often leave Chuck with relatives in Detroit, Kansas City, and Welby, Colorado. Chuck did enjoy his time in Colorado with his aunt and uncle. He had a dog there and always talked about how much he loved the beauty and freedom there—at least until his dog was killed. (Around the anniversary date of Chuck's death, I wanted to travel to Welby to understand what he felt that made him so happy. But Covid stopped me).

The students liked Chuck, but many people in the Pine Crest administration and many of the parents did not like him because of his Hoffa and mob connections. I got along fine at Pine Crest, however. I was the Lower School President of the Mothers Club in 1978–79 and later the Upper School President; the Chair of the Fashion Show in 1979–1980; and the Chair of the Book Fair in 1980–1981. I raised money for disabled children and made the lower school safer with a new pickup driveway.

During this period, I also was Program Director for the Florida Cystic Fibrosis Fashion Show. Jerry Weintraub, a film producer and friend of Chuck's, helped us get coverage in *USA Today*, magazines, and local newspapers. The University of Miami School of Medicine Board of Overseers gave our charity a Helping Hands Award for this program.

We moved from Inverrary to a small apartment in Plantation, Florida, near where my father was, around 1979. One day Chuck took me to a piece of property in Jacaranda, a golf community in Plantation, Florida. The view was breathtaking. It was on a lake, across from the eighteenth-hole green and the clubhouse. He said he was going to buy it for me.

I asked how he was going to do that since we were practically broke. He told me he was going to withdraw his Teamsters pension early to pay for it. Chuck hired a local builder, and we built a beautiful house. Of course, Chuck had bad luck even about this great home. Elvis died on August 15, 1975. But the newspaper headline the next day was not about Elvis. It was about Chuckie O'Brien having built a home with bulletproof glass and using non-union labor.

We enjoyed our Jacaranda home, which had a beautiful pool and pool fountain, and a boat dock with a great view across a lake. The boys loved the new home. They had fun in the pool. Brett would fish from the deck morning, noon, and night. The boys loved watching and throwing rocks at the alligators in the lake from the dock. I would repeat over and over to please be careful. I worried that Brett was going to get too close to the alligators. The boys would also go out on the golf course and throw the football.

Me and the boys at our Jacaranda home

Steven would be a bystander but enjoyed being with his brothers. Steven loved the water. To entertain him, I bought him a piano. Tony Provenzano, a leading suspect in the Hoffa disappearance and a friend of Chuck's, gave the boys a pool table. We put it in the garage, and the boys enjoyed it. I also remember the boys having friends over and Chuck cooking lots of big meals for them.

Our happy time at Jacaranda came to an end when Chuck went to jail in 1979. As part of the pressure put on all the Hoffa suspects, the government accused Chuck of falsifying bank loan applications and violating labor laws. He was sentenced to a year in prison and spent most of it at Eglin Air Force base in northern Florida.

Before Chuck went to Eglin, he was held at a detention center in Miami. I visited him there with Mother and Bertha—my first experience with a prison. I was able to visit Chuck, surrounded by inmates. He told me that they checked his bottom after making him get naked for anything he could be hiding. He was really very upset about that experience.

Chuck used his pension to build our dream house, but we still had to take out a mortgage to pay for the balance. Unfortunately, when Chuck went to prison, we no longer had an income to make the monthly payments. To deal with this problem, I called a man who, Chuck told me, would help if I ever needed anything. I do not remember his name, but I met him once at the country club at Jacaranda for lunch. "What did Chuck mean when he said you would help me?" I asked him. The man was noncommittal. He barely talked. I told the man I was having trouble making payments on the house, but he did not offer to help.

I then asked Mother to help make the payments. She said she couldn't help anymore. My brother Louis Jack was pressuring her, because any money Mother gave me would have come from Pancho's, and he did not want Pancho's paying for my house. He would complain to me and Mother every time she helped me. That is when I decided to put the house up for sale, about one year after we moved in. I would rather be on the streets than deal with these pressures. I sold the home quickly.

It was during this period—after Chuck had gone to prison, and after we sold the Jacaranda house, but before we moved out—that I started to not get along with my oldest son, Jack. He was a junior in high school and wanted to celebrate with his classmates and stay out all night at the house of one of his friends. At first, I said, "No," because Jack would be in his car driving on I-95. I finally relented but told him he first needed to pack up his room for the move out of the house.

Jack ignored me. On top of that, I had a confrontation with his girlfriend, whom I liked. I asked her and Jack to not mess up the house and to put away anything they used in the kitchen. They did not listen, and I got upset. After a while I got fed up with Jack and told him to leave the house and not come back. After Jack left for his event, I pulled everything out of his closet and threw it all on his bed. When he and his girlfriend returned the next day, she told Jack I was crazy. I don't think anyone likes to be called "crazy" after having shock treatments. But I knew that I was fine; the shock treatments had helped me.

After I sold the house, we moved to an apartment in Palm Aire in Pompano Beach. The boys helped me move. We lived there and managed our lives until Chuck got out of prison in January 1980. Chuck had booked an interview with Tom Snyder in New York, and I met him there. I was excited to see him, and we had a great time before returning home.

As soon as Chuck got home, he started work again with the Teamsters. He worked hard and was on the road a lot. Soon after he got home, I noticed that my stomach was hurting. I saw many doctors, and they told me I had an immune-deficiency disease and treated me with steroids. But the pain continued. Then I read in the newspaper about a doctor in Dallas named Ray who was an expert in immune-deficiency diseases. I went to Dallas and had a series of allergy tests, and then he admitted me to an environmental control center. I had more tests, and he concluded that I had a divided pancreas—something I was born with.

I had an operation on my pancreas in Dallas to close the divide in my pancreas. I later learned that while I was still in post-operation care, Chuck kissed another woman who was rolled out of surgery on her way to her room. He mistakenly thought it was me. He felt terrible. Her husband was standing nearby and was not happy with Chuck.

While I was in the hospital recovering from surgery, the boys visited me from Florida. They had been living mostly by themselves in Florida since I was in Dallas, and Chuck was visiting me and working on the road. The boys' football coach, Bill Munsey, and his wife, Jane, lived in the same high-rise apartment complex as we did—Palm Aire. Chuck arranged for the Munseys to check in on and watch over the boys. Sometimes they drove the boys to school.

When the boys visited me in the hospital in Dallas, Steven showed me a picture of him winning some certificate in school. In the picture I saw what seemed like a long white shirt sticking out of his green jacket. I asked why he had such a large shirt on. He said that it was not a shirt—it was a cast. He had broken his wrist while I was away, and no one had told me about it. Steven also told me that Jack had sawed it off with a knife before the boys visited me in Dallas so that I would not worry when I saw them.

A few months after I returned home, my oldest son, Jack, went to college at Washington & Lee University. And soon after that, we moved from Palm Aire to a townhouse in L'Ambiance, a community in Boca Raton, Florida. These were pretty good years. The FBI was still hounding Chuck—he would often see them and go talk to them outside our home in Boca—but the Hoffa story was not in the headlines. In 1981, the movie *Absence of Malice* came out. The lead character, Michael Gallagher, was based on Chuck's life and was played by Paul Newman. It was a story about someone whose life was ruined after he was wrongly framed by the press for killing a union official.

Chuck and the boys in the early 1980s

When my son Jack went to college he eventually grew apart from Chuck. Soon after he graduated in May 1984, he changed his name from "O'Brien" back to "Goldsmith," and, within a few years, he stopped talking to Chuck. Jack later explained in a book he wrote that he decided to break from Chuck because he worried his mob associations and connections to the Hoffa disappearance would affect his career and perhaps his safety.

I could not believe the downside of Jack's actions. I was hurt, Chuck was distraught, and life was not the same. We adjusted, although almost every day Chuck would say, "I just don't understand what I did to Jack. I love him as if he were my own son." Throughout Chuck's life, he was always concerned about Jack.

During the 1980s, Chuck and I had fun. Chuck's job was pretty steady and relatively quiet. We monitored Chuck's heart closely since he'd had a major heart operation years earlier. But his heart seemed to be fine at L'Ambiance. We walked a lot together for many miles and were pretty fit. I got skinny and looked anorexic, which didn't bother me because I preferred thin to overweight. I hired Rod Cortizo, a professional trainer, to work out with Chuck and me. Chuck loved the special attention and loved talking to Rod about soccer.

Chuck and I went on at least six cruises together. We took Mother on two or three of them with us. We spent a lot of our time with the boys. Brett was a great football player at Pine Crest, and Chuck was close with his coaches. Brett graduated from Pine Crest in 1984 and went to college at the University of Pennsylvania. Steven and I were always close, but, especially, after Brett left, we spent a lot of time together. He was great in the arts in Pine Crest, especially in the theater, where he had leading parts in many plays. Steven graduated from Pine Crest in 1987 and went to Yale for college.

In the mid-1980s, while Steven was still in high school, Chuck was involved in a dangerous situation. I received a phone call at home from Pat, the Secretary of Chuck's Teamsters boss, Joe Morgan. She told me, "Brenda, Chuck is with me, and he has to stay off of the streets. He wanted me to call you and let you know. I am coming to your home in Boca to explain what is going on."

Pat arrived an hour later and told me Chuck was in trouble in connection with a labor scheme in Miami related to the movie industry. Apparently, a mid-level mob figure in Chicago was not happy because he was not receiving payments. This person threatened Chuck, and

Chuck had to lay low at Pat's apartment. Chuck never spoke to me during this whole ordeal, which I didn't appreciate. I was left out in the cold. But I held it together. Thank goodness for shock treatments.

Chuck and me during happy times, on a cruise

I decided to leave town. I told Pat to tell Chuck I would be getting on a plane as soon as possible and would touch base when I arrived in Memphis with Steven. Steven was always such a trouper and so grown up, then and throughout his life. He did not question why we were leaving so quickly. Heaven only knows what was going through Steven's mind.

As we walked out of the locked house with luggage to go to the airport, I realized that Pat told me that Chuck said to be careful. I did not touch the car and told Steven to get a broom from the house. I took the broom and told Steven to get far away from the car. I hit the driver's door as hard as I could and then backed away quickly. I remembered the news about the car of the son of Teamsters' President Frank Fitzsimmons being blown to pieces in 1975.

Of course, our car did not blow to pieces. I felt lucky. People would later laugh when I told them the story about how I used the broom to check for a bomb. But I felt very safe and took that broom all the way to the Palm Beach airport. We flew to Memphis. Mother was concerned but quiet as always. She was the best mother in the world as far as I was concerned. Always there! Chuck finally called me in Memphis that night. He said everything was OK and that he was home. I came home the next day because Steven had to go to school.

When I got home, I was not happy with Chuck because he did not warn me about the threat—he had Pat do it. I was also worried about my safety and Steven's safety going forward. Chuck said this was a part of his life and he did what he had to do and could not talk to me. Chuck said that everything was safe, but I remained on guard and worried.

Chuck still had the stigma of being the number-one suspect in the Hoffa disappearance, both in the newspapers and in the Teamsters Union, where he was often shunned. He could not let the past go; being accused of hurting Hoffa ate at him every day of his life. He felt let down by everyone, but he still loved the Teamsters and worked hard for them.

From a young age, he had wanted to be president of Local 299 in Detroit, but that dream ended when Hoffa disappeared and Chuck moved to Florida. Sadly, Chuck never rose above the position of union organizer.

Chuck relaxing

Chuck was always so giving. He would help anyone—his family, his beloved Teamsters, his adopted relatives, a stranger, really anyone.

Most importantly, he was a savior in helping me with my boys. He was a true, genuine father, there for the boys at any time. He also managed to bring other families into his cocoon. He was so aware of all families and their needs, regardless of what his relationship was with them.

At times Chuck's generosity got the best of him. He would often promise more than he could deliver, and he often spent more than he had. Along with his many good and generous qualities, Chuck had some bad ones: he repeated himself, he frequently did not tell the truth, and he would buy things on my credit without being able to pay. I loved him and was upset with him—all at the same time.

Sometimes Chuck would use the Teamsters as if it were his own business—kind of like Hoffa did when he ran the union. Once, after several local police officers were killed just north of West Palm Beach, Chuck put on a fundraising event for the surviving families. He used Teamsters funds and a Teamsters airplane to fly in many entertainers for the event, including Waylon Jennings, Carl Perkins, and others. Mother and Daddy and I were all there. It was a great turnout. Chuck got Daddy, who had suffered a stroke, and brought him to the stage to meet Carl Perkins, whom Daddy had known many years earlier. Here we go again. Daddy was in his element—back into the Plantation Inn days of "Having Fun with Morris." Finally, Chuck managed to get Daddy off the stage so the show could start.

A few years later, in 1987, I divorced Chuck. I got a call from my brother Louis Jack who told me I had to divorce Chuck because my marriage to him would ruin Pancho's. Louis Jack worried that the mob would do something to Pancho's, and that if I divorced Chuck, it would take the pressure off. Louis Jack put pressure on

Mother, and I did not want to upset her, especially since she was helping with our income; I didn't want to be responsible for the downfall of Pancho's.

So, I told Chuck I needed to get a divorce. He got very, very sad. More than sad—really down. And then he started pressuring me. "Why are you doing this to me?" he asked, over and over. "What do you want me to do? The livelihood of our family depends on it," I said. I never thought the piece of paper for marriage meant anything. We got the divorce but, at this point, kept living together.

In 1991, Chuck's career with the Teamsters Union ended. Rudy Giuliani, the head federal prosecutor in New York, brought a controversial racketeering case against the Teamsters Union. He won a court case and set up a system to investigate and expel from the union anyone who "knowingly associated" with organized crime figures.

Chuck knew lots of people associated with the mafia—because of his mother's influence, he had grown up in that world. This was one of the main reasons he was kicked out of the Teamsters Union—because he knew these people. Another reason was alleged misspending of Teamsters Union funds.

Chuck started to go downhill after he was kicked out of the Teamsters. He acted on the outside as if nothing bothered him, but, inside, he was tortured about his life going off track. He was always stressed on the inside, and this would later lead to health problems. During this period, he started sweating profusely. He would be a little disoriented and not really the calm, together Chuck O'Brien he was when we first got married. He looked pale. Chuck went to the doctor and was diagnosed with diabetes, from which he would suffer his entire life. If you have the beginning stages of diabetes, be serious about treating it.

After he was kicked out of the Teamsters, Chuck got heavily involved in the Homeowners Association at L'Ambiance, where we lived. He was president for two terms. But some of the men in the community organized against him, saying he was associated with the mob in the newspapers and had served time in prison. It seemed as if Chuck's place in life was dwindling, and I could not stand it.

That is when I stepped in to support him. I put on an event to try to bring all homeowners together. I went to the meetings and made posters. Chuck believed his opponents were breaking the rules and skimming money from the association. He also did not like their plans for the community. I was upset by how they treated Chuck, but he never opened his mouth or opposed their efforts. I organized the community against them and helped elect a woman as president of the L'Ambiance Homeowners Association, who was excellent.

Sometime in the early 1990s, Geneva Goldsmith, Jack Jr.'s mother, was institutionalized in Little Rock. She was an alcoholic and was found wandering the streets half naked. My sons Brett and Steven flew to Little Rock. They had never met their grandmother before but showed up to prevent her from being institutionalized. Jack Jr. also showed up, hoping to gain control of Geneva and get control of her money. (He did not realize she was broke.)

On the day of the hearing, Jack Jr. approached Steven, who was sitting near the front of the room. He told him he had on a nice suit and asked if he was Geneva's lawyer. "No, I am your son," he said. This is the worst Jack Jr. story of all of Jack Jr. stories. He did not recognize his own flesh and blood.

The judge discharged Geneva to Brett's care after he pledged to make sure she was taken care of until she got better and out of her alcoholic state. Brett immediately called me and said he needed help with Geneva, and Geneva reached out to me also.

Life is truly a merry-go-round. Geneva had never been nice to me and never liked me, since my marriage to Jack Jr. had disrupted her life. But I agreed to help her. She arrived, and I took her to a doctor. Geneva had bags of medicine she was taking. The doctor told her she was taking enough drugs to kill a horse. She laughed, and the doctor weaned her off the medicine. Geneva stayed with us three months, and when she left, she was walking every day, her mind was clear, and she was happy to be on the mend.

Chuck was a trouper with Geneva. He played canasta with us—I had no idea he could even play cards. During one game, he excused himself, went to his closet, and returned with a wooden nickel, which he threw on the table. "Here, this is what I owe you," Chuck said. Geneva laughed, and she loved it. That blew my mind. I just shook my head, thinking, *What else will happen as life unfolds?*

Chapter 16

Life After the Teamsters

The year after Chuck was kicked out of the Teamsters, a movie came out called *Hoffa*. Jimmy Hoffa was played by Jack Nicholson. Danny DeVito produced and directed the movie. He also played Bobby Ciaro, Hoffa's sidekick. The character was based on Chuck.

Brett tried to make a deal with DeVito to use a screenplay that he developed, but it did not work out. Chuck thought the movie was "bullshit"—the script was fictional, and Nicholson was no good as Hoffa. He always gave running commentary about movies about Hoffa. He said the actor who played Hoffa the best was Robert Blake, in the 1983 film *Blood Feud*.

The next January, in 1993, Chuck went on the *Maury Povich Show* to try to clear his name. "I am tired of headlines coming out in this country saying that I drove this man to his death," he told Maury. "I have had it; I have got a family, and it's destroyed them." Maury then asked Chuck if he took Hoffa "in a car unwittingly to a meeting with 'some connected people' in Detroit?" Chuck denied it and said he would be willing to "take a lie detector test on your program, conducted by whoever you want to bring in here, about where I was that day." I was so upset when Chuck agreed to do this, because, if he made a mistake on national television, he would have been in trouble.

Maury got Natale Laurendi, the New York Police Department's "star lie detector," according to the *New York Times*. Laurendi conducted the test and, on the following week's show, announced that Chuck had passed. "As far as I'm concerned, he was telling the truth when he claimed he was not in an automobile with James Hoffa on the afternoon of July 30, 1975."

My brother Louis Jack died on June 19, 1993. A few days later Chuck and I moved from Boca Raton to Memphis. We lived in Mother's beautiful townhome in Memphis. Mother fired the president of Pancho's and made me the president. For the next seven years or so, I worked morning, noon, and night for the company.

Louis Jack's will named me as the executrix of his estate. That means my brother designated me to protect the assets in his estate and make distributions of property to his beneficiaries. Soon a big lawsuit ensued. Morris, Jack, and my brother's wife, Sylvia, tried to have me removed as the executrix, but after an eight-day hearing, the judge rejected their request. At that point, Mother filed a lawsuit against the estate. She claimed that Louis Jack had fraudulently induced her into transferring her Pancho's stock to him before his death. The estate also had many outstanding claims against it. Years of court appearances followed. In the end, a settlement resolved the case.

The years of lawsuit proceedings took a toll on everyone, especially Mother. One of the saddest days in my life was when the judge made Mother—in her mid-80s, and in a wheelchair—wait from around noon until almost 10:00 p.m. to testify. She, as always, was a trouper and stuck it out, even when she had to testify against members of her family.

Me and Mother in Memphis, when I was running Pancho's

That must have broken her heart, but she never mentioned it afterwards. She kept her feelings inward. I would love to know the secret to her strength. I think it was because she was a youngest child, had to take care of herself at a young age, was alone with her mother when she died, lost a young daughter, had a father who spent time in prison, married into an orthodox Jewish family at a young age, and had a difficult marriage. She was tough.

Before this lawsuit ended, in 1995, my best girlfriend Toni Wiley and I went to my home in Boca Raton for a little break. Chuck was not in town. I settled in early one evening and was almost asleep when the doorbell rang. Toni went to the door and asked who it was. The answer was that it was the FBI with a letter for Chuck. I told her to ask the agents to leave the letter outside. About 30 minutes later, I got the letter and opened it. It was written by FBI agent Andrew Sluss, who asked to meet with Chuck about the Hoffa disappearance. He said, "I do not consider you a suspect in this matter." This statement left me elated. Chuck finally had an admission from the FBI that he was innocent of anything that had to do with Mr. Hoffa.

I brought the letter back to Memphis and showed it to Chuck. He had no expression on his face but shook his head like it wasn't a big deal. He thought the letter was a joke or a set-up. Inside I think he was happy. I kept asking him why he wasn't happier that the whole thing was over. I said, "It is over, and you can start a new life." He said, "No, it will never be over with them. My reputation is what it is, and it will never change." I told him to have faith that the tide was turning. He said he wished he could believe it, but he didn't.

When I returned to Memphis, the local news did a story on one of the Pancho's restaurants, and they wanted to include the family and anyone else who was part of Pancho's through the years. Toward the end of the show, Mother was interviewed. During the interview, she looked straight at one of the past employees in the corporate offices of Pancho's who was there. "You were a terrible employee of Pancho's, and you were lazy," she said. Mother always spoke her mind.

While I was president, Pancho's won the "Taste of the Town" Award. Mother attended the ceremony with me and was very proud and very emotional. I was also twice included in the "Memphis 50 Women of the Year Who Made a Difference in the Mid-South" awarded by *Memphis Woman* magazine.

Chuck backdoored me a lot when I ran Pancho's. He would try to help me, and he helped me get our cheese dip into grocery stores, but he usually screwed things up. I would make a decision, and he would bring in another idea without discussion, as if it were *his* business. He had no respect for the burden I was carrying—trying to save the business, dealing with lawyers, my mother's health, employees, a lack of money to run the business, and much more. The finances were so bad that I had to put the company's cheese purchases on my credit card. It was a never-ending battle, and I was really getting tired.

Instead of helping, which I know Chuck was trying to do, he was hindering my ability to run the company. So, I had to get Chuck out of my life for a while. I asked him to leave—I could not deal with him *and* Pancho's. He stayed with a friend in Mississippi and started seeing a psychiatrist. Chuck wrote me this note:

To My Darling Brenda Lou,

You are my heart's twin, my first thought in the morning and my last thought at night.

You are my soul's mirror, the only one who truly understands how it is with me. I wish I could put into words the depth of my feelings for you. When I think about the good times (like last week) we've shared, and, yes, the most difficult ones I have put you through! But I guess my love for you—I just loved and tried too hard. I had never known how bad I hurt you until you told me that on Saturday night. It hurts so much that Brett, Steven, and Jack feel that I hurt you. Much of my life, I tried so hard to do right.

But I don't think I am good for me or anyone I love. I feel simply and quietly grateful to have found you. But I was never— in your eyes—what you are looking for in a man. I want you to know this is my last letter, note, or card—it means so much to me to be giving it to you. I want you to have a super XMAS with the ones you love so much.

Both before and after Chuck left, Bob Rivet had been calling me a lot. On one call, he told me he was going to Nashville. I said that I was, too—to meet a kitchen designer. We met in the lobby of the bar at the new Grand Old Opry. Bob was wearing a toupee. Bob told me I looked beautiful. We went to another bar outside by the pool. We had a nice dinner together, and then Bob dropped me off at my room; nothing happened. He called me the next morning to say goodbye. It was good to see him.

When I got back to Memphis, Chuck came to visit me one night, and we talked. He started crying, which broke my heart. He told me about the psychiatrist and said she gave him several assignments. Here is a letter about one assignment:

To My Brenda Lou:

The doctor gave me an assignment to read a book she had that included 25 sayings that I could read and use in everyday life. She said that I should also give you my list so that you could see how much you mean to me in my life.

With love always, Chuck.

1. Make a list of twenty-five things you want to experience before you die. Carry it in your wallet, and refer to it often.

2. Worry makes for a hard pillow. When something is troubling you when you're going to bed for the night, jot down three things you can do the next day to help solve the problem.

3. Spend your life lifting people up—not putting people down.

4. Keep a tight rein on your temper.

5. Make the punishment fit the crime.

6. Never deprive anyone—it may be all that they have.

7. Never take action when you are angry.

8. Don't use time or words carelessly. Neither can be retrieved.

9. For the next twenty-four hours, refrain from criticizing anybody or anything.

10. Admit your mistakes.

11. Avoid negative people.

12. Don't carry a grudge.

13. Everything you say and do is a reflection of the inner you.

14. Chuck becomes successful the moment Chuck starts moving toward a worthwhile goal.

15. The future belongs to those who believe in the beauty of their dreams.

16. The key to happiness is having dreams. The key to success is making dreams come true.

17. Do not follow where the path may lead. Go, instead, where there is no path, and leave a trail.

18. Persistence prevails when all else fails.

19. The difference between ordinary and extraordinary is the little extra.

20. Become the most positive and enthusiastic person you know.

21. Far away, there is the sunshine and my highest aspirations. I may not reach them, but I can look up and see their beauty, believe in them, and try to follow where they lead.
22. Give yourself a year, and read the Bible cover to cover.
23. Every so often, watch *Sesame Street*.
24. Brenda Lou, remember that, in life, the most important thing is trust.
25. Never give up on Brenda Lou—miracles happen every day.

This all upset me very much. I didn't like to see him so sad. I told him he could come back to the house.

I decided we needed a break. We took a road trip to Greer's Ferry and stayed on the Lake at Heber Springs in Arkansas. On the way there, I told him I had seen Bob and exactly what happened. "I know," he said. I never asked how he knew.

We had a great time at Heber Springs. It was great to be away from work and pressure. I told Chuck how badly he had hurt me by backdooring me at Pancho's and by being unreliable with money and other matters. But I also told him how much I loved him. We both thought our different journeys—mine with Pancho's and Chuck's with his work and troubles—had caused us to drift apart. But we also had a deep love for each other. We knew that our love was very, very deep and that we would always be there for each other. This was true, no matter the circumstances. Our time together at Heber Springs allowed us to regroup and recommit to our relationship.

We took our time going back to Memphis since I wanted to stop by some of the antique stores in Arkansas, which were awesome. I found a lot of great things for my son Steven, who had graduated from Yale Law School and was moving to Los Angeles.

After our trip to Heber Springs, Chuck wrote the following. (Chuck wrote me so many things during his lifetime, but, for some reason I never really absorbed what he was telling me until after he died). Here is what he wrote:

To Someone Close to My Heart

Close to my heart are my memories of you. You make my life brighter—and happier, too.

Close to my heart are all the things you've done—the good times we've shared, along with the bad, for which I am so sorry. You and the boys always are a wonderful part of my life.

Brenda Lou, I'll always keep you so close to my heart.

With love,
Chuck

One of the best things that happened to me and Chuck in Memphis was a dog we discovered in a Mexican pot near the front door of Pancho's offices. The dog was part German Shepherd and part Collie. I brought her into our office because it was so cold. Our secretary, Pam Wallace, named the dog "Honey."

Honey stayed that night in the office but set off the alarm. I insisted on bringing Honey home the next day. We got her food and took her to the vet. Honey was pregnant and had nine puppies a month later. We gave them all away except for one, whom I named "Sweetie." I loved Sweetie, but Chuck later backdoored me by giving her away without telling me. But we kept Honey. She loved Chuck and was by his side when he was sick. Honey was a constant companion of ours until she died at the age of twenty-two.

In 1999, we sold Mother's house in Memphis and moved back to Florida. Steven moved to Memphis to run Pancho's. Chuck and I and Honey drove down to Boca Raton together. Chuck loved road trips and especially with Honey, and Honey loved road trips especially with Chuck. She loved being by his side and loved her new home when she arrived in Boca Raton.

After I got back to Boca Raton, I took a break and went to Mii Amo, a resort in the red rocks of Sedona, Arizona. Its Native American name means "journey," reflecting the resort's philosophy of "achieving a transformation in physical health, emotional well-being, and spiritual renewal." The main thing that drew me to Mii Amo was the Apache Indians. I requested a private tour of the local mountains to learn the history of the Indians. I asked my guide, named George, a lot of questions during the tour. One was, "What should we do to live a full life with love and healing?" I wrote down his answer and still have the paper. He said: "Apache Healing 3 magic words. Create calm—calm creates clarity. Look at body to look at immune system and to give all the immune system a way to come back stronger to heal. Remember to swim the ocean of joy and love." I loved that answer. It was just what I needed.

George also told me that the Apache Indians were given land, but the government took it away to build a pipeline through it. He took me up to the top of the Red Rocks and showed me where the Indians had lived. There was a lot of writing and figures inscribed into the rock. I imagined a rock digging into the red rock. You could feel their presence, and I wondered about so many things, including how they climbed the rocks, how they survived, and how they had so much wisdom.

When I returned home, Mother flew down to Boca Raton to live with us. I got her settled in Steven's room. She could not walk and could barely stand up. She had a very weak heart. I got a nurse to take care of Mother. She did pretty well for the next six months. But then she developed fluid in her lungs. I got her a respiratory nurse. I also took her to the doctor, and he recommended a flu shot—something Mother had always avoided. But she said, "Yes" this time. When I went in to check on her the next day, on December 26, 1999, she was dead. We had a private funeral for her in Boca.

It was hard for me to understand that Mother was gone. She had always been by my side since I was born, and now she was gone. However, from the day she died, I always felt her presence with me.

Chapter 17

Music and Dancing

I grew up in music, and I had an interest in writing music from a young age. An important influence on my music writing was Goddard Lieberson, who was president of Columbia Records.

Mother met Goddard when she and I went on vacation in the late 1950s at the Americana Hotel in Miami Beach. Somehow, Mother met him by the pool. He invited her to his poolside cabana, and she asked me to join. We ate at his cabana villa. Goddard was handsome, cordial, and was very interested in Mother's stories about the Plantation Inn. I told Goddard I was interested in music. I could not sing or play an instrument, but I was interested in writing song lyrics. He was very cordial and gave us his business card.

A year or so later, I wrote Goddard, reminded him that we discussed music, and told him that I had an idea for a song about the Plantation Inn. I asked him if he could make it into a song. Goddard wrote me back a nice note on March 21, 1961:

Here is what the letter said:

Dear Brenda:

Of course, I remember you and your mother.

Let me say, first of all, about your song, that I'm afraid things don't work this way. You'll have to find somebody to write music for it to begin with, which, I don't have to tell you, is a very important part of the song. The next thing, I think, would be the interest of local artists in doing it, and possibly getting a recording artist interested. I can't tell you much more than that because the popular music world is now so peculiar and frenzied that it is difficult to know just how they operate. Furthermore, I am afraid that I see a very small part of it. If you really want to see how it works, you must take a little trip over to your neighbor, Nashville, Tennessee!

All best wishes to you and your mother.

Goddard Lieberson

Many decades later, I remembered Goddard's advice when I decided that I wanted to enter the music business. While I was in Memphis running Pancho's, I finally started writing a song, called *Music Filled My Soul*, about the Plantation Inn. Later, in Boca Raton, I found a company in Nashville that could write music to my lyrics. They developed nice tunes. So, I just kept writing song after song, and this company kept writing tunes. I have written eighteen songs altogether. I started entering songwriting contests and won many awards.

I also attended a songwriting retreat at the REO Rafting Resort outside of beautiful Vancouver, B.C. I learned about rhyme schemes and how to improve my music-writing skills. And I met many great artists, including Pam Tillis. Pam read a version of a song I wrote

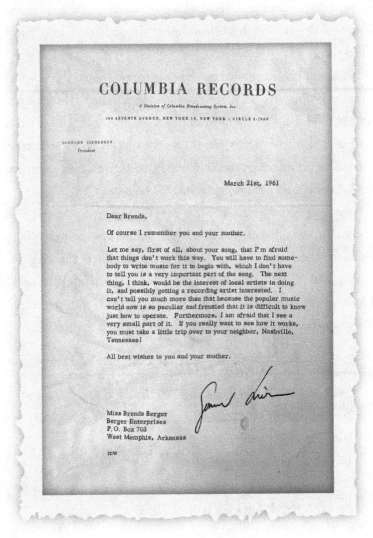

COLUMBIA RECORDS
A Division of Columbia Broadcasting System, Inc.

799 SEVENTH AVENUE, NEW YORK 19, NEW YORK · CIRCLE 5-7300

GODDARD LIEBERSON
President

March 21st, 1961

Dear Brenda,

Of course I remember you and your mother.

Let me say, first of all, about your song, that I'm afraid
that things don't work this way. You will have to find somebody to write music for it to begin with, which I don't have
to tell you is a very important part of the song. The next
thing, I think, would be the interest of local artists in doing
it, and possibly getting a recording artist interested. I
can't tell you much more than that because the popular music
world now is so peculiar and frenzied that it is difficult to know
just how to operate. Furthermore, I am afraid that I see a
very small part of it. If you really want to see how it works,
you must take a little trip over to your neighbor, Nashville,
Tennessee!

All best wishes to you and your mother.

Miss Brenda Berger
Berger Enterprises
P. O. Box 703
West Memphis, Arkansas

mw

Goddard Lieberson's letter to me

called "Two Kings," a song about Elvis Presley and Dr. Martin
Luther King. "I was intrigued with the idea because it was not the
ordinary 'love' or 'love gone wrong' kind of song you tend to hear

so much," Pam later said. "It was kind of audacious connecting the dots between two big historical figures. It made me think, and I liked that."

Pam and I corresponded on the song for two years. "Brenda was so excited by some of the suggestions I made that she just kinda made up her mind that I had to be involved," Pam once told George Klein during an interview. "And I imagine anyone who knows Brenda knows she is charming and not the kind of person to give up on a mission. And this song did become a mission, for both of us."

The song was released in 2012. Pam sang on it, and so did Kris Thomas, a Memphis singer I discovered online. I introduced him to Pam, and she thought he would be a great addition to the song. "As soon as I heard Kris's voice, though, I knew he was going to work. I loved everything about him, his fresh look, his God-given voice." They sang the song beautifully together. Here are the lyrics:

Two kings walked through Memphis
One had a dream, one had a song
But each man brought a message of love
That lives on and on and on
And though that Mississippi River
Can hardly hold our tears
The legacy they left us with
We'll treasure through the years
Remembering two kings

Well, they came up out of Tupelo
Shook the whole world up
With his jet-black hair and blue suede shoes

One look and it was love
And on that dark day at Graceland
When he went to join his mother
We knew we'd lost our rock and roll king
And there'll never be another

Two kings walked through Memphis
One had a dream, one had a song
Though they're walking with the angels now
The memories live on
And though that Mississippi River
Still flows with our tears
The legacy they left us with
We'll treasure through the years
Talking about two kings

He walked the streets of Memphis
With a Bible in his hand
And the kingdom that he dreamed of
Some couldn't understand
And with no more than a single shot
His work on Earth was done
But he showed us the way to the Promised Land
And we must keep marching on

There are thoughts that fly away
Set the world to light from dark
Songs and dreams are just like bridges
That connect heart to heart

When those years from up above
They're still bridges made of love.

Oh, he took us to the mountain
Whoa, he sang away our pain
Two kings gone yet the song and dream remain

Two kings walk through Memphis
Two kings touched our souls
One man had a vision
And one man came to rock and roll

And that Mississippi River
Still flows with our tears
Now they're just gonna carry on and
Celebrate the years
We spent with two kings
Whoa Oh oh oh oh
Remembering Celebrate oh oh oh

Pam introduced me to the documentary filmmaker Molly Secours, who produced the music video. It was shot in various historic Memphis locations, including Beale Street, the banks of the Mississippi River, and the Stax Music Academy. Boo Mitchell, the son of Willie Mitchell, whom I knew at the Plantation Inn, also lent his support to the project, as well as kids at the Stax Academy. Tim Sampson's help was vital. He is the communications director for the Soulsville Foundation, an organization that operates, among other things, the Stax Music Academy in Memphis. He opened the door at Stax for us to film some of the video. I was very proud of the song and the project. The video has been viewed more than 1.1 million times on YouTube.

I was very fortunate that three of my four grandchildren were musically gifted. Nicholas, Brett's oldest son, had an amazing talent for making rap beats and lyrics. He helped me a lot, especially on my anti-bullying song, "Remember." Christopher, Nicholas' brother, is a very talented pianist and composer. Williams, Jack's youngest son, is a very talented guitarist and songwriter. He sometimes added elements to my songs.

In 2014, I was stunned by the suicide of two Florida teens as a result of bullying. I decided to write a song about bullying. The song was called "Remember." I wanted to make it as powerful as I could, so I got almost a dozen people to sing on it. I was lucky enough to meet the great Rob Roy at Power Station Recording Studio in Pompano Beach. Rob produced the body of the song and "Boo" Mitchell at Willie Mitchell's Royal Studio in Memphis produced the beginning and the end, with Stax singers. (Tim Sampson helped again.) The video debuted in October 2014 at an event in Boca Raton, Florida. Rob Roy organized the event, and the Mayor of Boca Raton spoke there.

In November 2014, I signed up for a workout session with a girl who used the Fred Astaire studio. I went every day for two months. I grew interested in learning how to do a dance routine to one of my songs, and to learn ballroom dancing. The owner of the studio told me about a dance instructor named Kirill Hitroff. The only drawback, she told me, was that Kirill did not speak English well. I didn't care about that, and I signed up.

I did my homework and learned that Kirill had started ballroom dancing at age six in Odessa, Ukraine, and was later a Ukrainian

National Ballroom Champion, a "Dancing with the Stars" finalist in Ukraine, and a competitor all over Europe. He was also a finalist in the Blackpool ballroom dance competition—the most famous in the world. When I first met him, I was very impressed and felt extremely lucky to be in his presence. He took me by the hand and said, "Let's dance." We did my favorite dance, which, in my day, I called "The Jitterbug," but Kirill called it "The East Coast Swing."

Kirill and me dancing

Dancing with Kirill is so easy to follow. He swept me up and started a dance we had not even practiced. We entered many contests and won a trophy for the Vegas World Championship 2015 Performance Award, and another one the same year in Boston, the First Coast Classic Championship. (All of these awards were in my age group.) We had so much fun. Kirill has kept me young and excited about my life. I love music, but my second love is dancing, and Kirill filled that gap missing in my life.

Soon after my dancing tournaments, during the period when I was most productive writing songs and working on anti-bullying causes, I discovered that I had stage 4 lung cancer. I had been having headaches and got a brain scan. The brain scan accidentally picked up a spot on my lungs. I smoked a lot for the first half of my life, and that is probably why I got it. I had surgery to take two lobes out of one of my lungs. When I had my lung operation, I was surrounded by love. My three boys were there, and Chuck was there. The operation was a success, though I later had to have a second operation through my throat to remove more cancer.

Then I had to do radiation and chemotherapy. A cancer doctor explained to me in simple words what chemotherapy was and what its side effects were. Another doctor explained radiation and said I would feel the effects only at the end of the therapy, when I would receive a higher dose.

I was in a lot of pain as a result of these treatments. I could not swallow or eat without excruciating pain and had to have a stomach tube inserted to get medicine and nourishment. I went into semi-coma; my blood pressure shot up; and I had a slight stroke. And yet I was lucky and survived. My doctor was so worried that when I finally regained some strength and rebounded, he told me I had given him gray hair. He asked if I knew who he was. I called him "Memphis!" I could not think of his name, but I connected him to Memphis because, when I first met him, he told me he once lived in Memphis.

My son Steven stayed by my side during this ordeal. He moved to a place nearby that had a beautiful view of the water. Brett wanted him to have a water view so I could visit after I recovered and enjoy it. I was so grateful, when I got better, to know that Steven was there.

The doctor told me not to drive until I was off my pain medicine, so I immediately quit. That was a drastic mistake. I had horrible withdrawals—I had chills and was like a zombie, frozen and staring at the ceiling, yet shaking incessantly. *When will this end?* I thought. But it did finally end, and I felt better.

My next priority was to deal with my thinning hair. Steven drove me to Bal Harbor to find the lady who'd assisted my mother in the early '60s after she bleached her hair from her beautiful auburn color to a blonde. The lady I was looking for, Ruth Regina, was the top wig lady in America. Her salon was full of photos of the movie stars I admired. I found her after an interval of more than 40 years! She had different photos in her salon from the ones I remembered from four decades earlier. One in particular that was so gorgeous was of Jennifer Lopez. Ruth Regina once appeared on the David Letterman show and dressed up the doggies with her perfected wigs.

When I found Ruth, she said she remembered Mother. I left her with several hairpieces and knew I was in the best hands I could be in, thanks, once again to Mother, who was helping me even after she died. It was a wonderful feeling. I eventually got my hair back to normal and sent Wendy Moten one of the beautiful long-haired wigs for Wendy's gigs and stage performances. I was able to give something I had received, which, on my radar, was a blessing for me to do.

My doctor told me Chuck had to leave the house during my cancer treatments because he had a contagious skin disease. By this time, Chuck was in pretty bad shape. His diabetes had worsened. He could walk only with a walker and needed lots of attention from nurses. So, I told Chuck he needed to go to a rehab facility while I was going through treatment. He went bonkers, but he did it.

After I got better, Chuck moved back in, and I returned to music. I was so blessed during this period to meet Charles Calello and his lovely wife, Clay. I met them at the Power Station studio in Pompano Beach, where I was learning how to use the studio and produce songs. Charles is an arranger, composer, conductor, and producer. He has had 38 top 20 songs, including "Sweet Caroline" (sung by Neil Diamond), "Native New Yorker" (sung by Odyssey), and "My Heart Belongs to Me" (sung by Barbra Streisand).

Charles and Clay Calello

Clay and I had a lot in common, and we became friends right away. Charles produced three of my songs, which was a great honor for me. Charles and Clay also loved Chuck. Charles and Chuck would ride in the cart while golfing and tell stories. Everyone found Chuck interesting and thought he was a great storyteller, as well as a truly giving person, very funny, and, of course, a great bullshitter. We always had fun at dinners together.

Chapter 18

Chuck Passes

Chuck and I were living in Boca Raton when the September 11, 2001, attacks occurred. A few weeks earlier, Chuck received a visit from FBI agent Andrew Sluss. Sluss left a letter saying that he wanted to give Chuck a lie detector test so that he could clear his name. Chuck met and discussed the matter with the agents. But everyone in the family advised him against it, so he didn't. He was afraid the FBI was setting him up.

About this time, new allegations against Chuck about the Hoffa disappearance surfaced. Chuck got angry and decided to go on the Larry King show to defend himself. He knew King from his days with Hoffa. The show was scheduled for September 12, 2001. Chuck was set to fly out there on September 11. Chuck left on an American Airlines flight that morning and was supposed to change planes in Dallas. But after the 9-11 attacks, somewhere over New Orleans, the plane turned around and went to Tampa. Chuck rented a van because there were no cars to rent. He brought back six passengers to Ft. Lauderdale. He called me from there and said he was on his way home and helping passengers with a ride.

After my son Jack had his first child, Jack IV, he and his sweet wife, Leslie, and the baby came to visit us in Boca Raton. This was the first time that Jack had seen Chuck since he broke with him in college. Jack was still cool to Chuck on this trip, and Chuck was still hurt and disappointed, as was I. However, a few years later, Jack visited with his family again. By this time, Jack IV was three years old and he had a baby brother, Williams. On this trip, Jack apologized to Chuck for breaking with him decades earlier and for being distant during that time. They grew close again and would write a book together. Time took care of things, just as I said it would.

Me and Chuck, my boys, and their families at Sea Island, Georgia

On this trip, Jack got extremely upset when Honey barked at the boys, and his son Jack, who was afraid of dogs, started crying. He asked me to take Honey somewhere so that his son would not be upset. I told him that Honey would not bother him and that he would get used to Honey. Time always takes care of fear or obstacles along our way. Before long, his two sons were playing with Honey and throwing Honey's toys for her to go after. They were laughing as time went by, and there were no tears in their beautiful eyes.

Starting around 2012, Jack and Chuck started writing a book about Chuck and his life with Hoffa. They spent many hundreds of hours together in discussion and interviews. I joined them for many of them. Jack asked a lot of questions, but Chuck tended to deflect the questions he did not want to answer. Some of the conversations were very funny, as Jack and Chuck are very different people.

Chuck talked to his family—his daughter, Josephine, his son, Chuckie, and their families—at least once each week. They lived in Kansas City, Missouri. He loved his conversations with them, and he especially loved it when they visited us in Boca Raton.

Chuck's family and close friends

As time progressed Chuck lost many friends to death, and his own health started on a downward path. When Chuck got into his mid-80s, he found out he had cancer of the esophagus. We went to Cleveland Clinic to have him evaluated by a doctor he really respected. The doctor had to conduct several treatments—four operations in all.

The doctor told Chuck that the last treatment would make him very uncomfortable for quite a while, like a sunburn in his throat. Chuck was more than uncomfortable; he was in excruciating pain. This pain defeated the last bit of drive that Chuck had within him. Even swallowing was horrible. He had medicines to coat his throat, but nothing helped. Each day he was getting weaker. His doctor said he would have to tolerate it for a little while longer.

Chuck's diabetes was also growing worse. He had been suffering from this disease for decades, but by his eighties, it was really taking over. Chuck did not always eat like he was supposed to, and he did not get enough exercise. It got harder and harder for him to walk. And he did something I never thought I would see: he stopped driving. People came to the house to try to get him to get out and do things, but he was usually in too much pain.

Jack's book about Chuck, *In Hoffa's Shadow*, came out in September 2020. Jack used all of his knowledge and investigative ability to clear Chuck of the 45-year-old accusation that he was involved in Hoffa's disappearance. At first, Chuck was down about the book because Jack portrayed Chuck's role in the Teamsters Union honestly, including some of Chuck's shortcomings as a labor organizer and the reasons Hoffa never promoted him in the union. Chuck had a much higher view of his role in the union and was disappointed, since he had tried hard all of his life to help people in the union.

But when the book started to get great reviews, he cheered up. He could not believe it when, after years of negative stories and being falsely accused of involvement in the Hoffa disappearance, major news outlets started saying that he was innocent and was a great man and a great father, despite his missteps. He called Jack and told him how grateful he was for the book.

But Chuck's happiness did not last long. He was in enormous pain with his throat and his diabetes. The filmmaker Errol Morris wanted to interview Chuck about his life for a possible movie. The crew came to our home in Boca Raton. Chuck was in terrible pain during the day of the filming—too much pain to even think. He did not answer the questions well. The stress was way too much for him. After two grueling days, Chuck and I, and Jack and his son Jack IV, went to a nice dinner at one of Chuck's favorite Italian restaurants.

Within a couple of weeks, Chuck had hit bottom. I asked him if he would like to go for a ride with me for a doctor's appointment. He perked up and said, "Yes." He was unusually enthusiastic—almost strangely so. I got the car ready as his nurse Tarsia put him in his wheelchair. Chuck told Tarsia, "Tell Brenda Lou I am coming"—just as he told me years ago, when I was at a low point, that he was coming to West Memphis to help me.

Just after he said that, he slumped over in his chair with an ashen look. Tarsia caught him, gently put him on the ground, and started CPR. I was talking to him, and so was Tarsia. He was not responding. We called 911, and they arrived quickly. I still had the car keys in my hand; a police officer came up and asked for the keys to the car. I asked, "Why?" and he insisted he needed the keys to my car. I gave them to him and then answered the questions for the paramedics.

The paramedics began a machine CPR on Chuck and then took him to the ambulance. They did not allow me to go with Chuck. Before the ambulance left, the paramedic asked if he could give Chuck a light sedative because he was fighting their attempt to put a tube in his throat. I did not like the idea, but they insisted, and I agreed.

The ambulance left for the hospital. The police officer was still at my house and would not let me leave to go to the hospital. I was beside myself. Chuck was not dead as far as I knew, and I wanted to be with him. The police officer kept on and on with the paperwork. He was so slow. I finally told him he had to question me at the hospital.

He allowed me to leave just minutes after I got the call that Chuck had passed. I rushed to the hospital, and they let me be in the room with his body. I talked to him for what seemed like an eternity, but, eventually, they told me they had to put him into a body bag and that I had to leave. I was glad, because I do not think I could have looked at that. I was in shock. In my heart, I knew that Chuck would always be with me, and I never thought about death.

Chuck was my rock from the day we got together, and for more than half of my life. I miss him every day. I was blessed deeply by God to have him come into my life. He was a giving man, and he had a loving heart. He is gone but will always be in my heart and memories.

I had to arrange Chuck's funeral, which Steven helped me do. All of Chuck's family and close friends were there. He would have been happy that so many people he loved showed up. Rob Roy helped me with the songs. I buried Chuck next to my mother in a mausoleum near my home.

Chapter 19

And Then
There Was David

The Covid lockdown came just a few weeks after Chuck passed. Suddenly I was stuck in the house and lonelier than I had ever been in my life. I had new realizations—and new vulnerabilities.

Throughout my life, I had given to others. After Chuck passed, I could not give of myself anymore. But I came to realize something important about Chuck's love for me: He was always very loving, but because of my prior husbands and experiences with other men, it was hard for me to believe or trust him, and I never fully opened my heart to him. After he died, this realization made me sad. The lesson I learned is to open your heart fully to someone you love and trust.

Unfortunately, the lesson I learned about opening my heart led to other, different, problems. Less than a month after Chuck passed, I was on Facebook. A distinguished, good-looking, middle-aged man whom I would later know as David had posted at least five professional photos of himself on my page. When I opened one up, a photo of me came up next to his.

Of course, this drew my attention and curiosity. *What if I open the next photo of him?* Yes, there was a different photo of me. I was really curious and clicked on all the photos. Every time, there was a picture of me next to him. One of the photos was a picture of me and my boys that was one of my favorites. When I later returned to the site, neither David's pictures nor mine were there. I had pulled two of his photos to save copies before he pulled them off of Facebook. I wondered how this man got onto my Facebook page and was able to do whatever he wanted on my page.

I immediately shared David's photos with my sons and recounted what had happened. Steven texted me that his photos were a scam and advised me to stay away from him. Steven asked me to share the photos and the episode with a friend to see what she would say. He predicted that she would tell me it was a scam. Steven was right. But it was too late. I was consumed with a new freedom—and hooked on David.

A little while after David's pictures disappeared from my Facebook page, I got an email from David. I am not sure how he got my address. He told me his last name, but it was a Middle Eastern name that I could not pronounce or remember. Then he posted his American name, and said he'd grown up in America. He said he was in the United States to contact a friend but was having problems locating him. He said he loved my photos and was drawn to them. I asked him why he was drawn to my page out of the millions of Facebook pages.

Of course, I thought about the odd coincidence of Chuck's death and David's arrival. But I was drawn to David on Facebook, and now he was somehow inside my emails. In case you think your privacy is protected by Facebook and that, when you post information, it is shared only with your friends, you are wrong. David had all the freedom he wanted, not as a Facebook friend but as my Facebook enemy.

As my psychologist later told me, I was vulnerable to David because I was trying to fill the holes in my heart, the spaces that had not been filled. David appeared at a time in which I was at my most vulnerable. I missed Chuck, I was stuck alone in the house with Covid lockdown, and suddenly I had someone who seemed to care about me. I was craving and wanting to receive love and was finally ready once I realized I had lost Chuck and so much of his love. David took advantage of me.

At first, David told me he was in the northeastern United States "looking for a special person." He was very mysterious about who this special person was. Then one day, he sent me a photo by email. It was a young man about the age of my youngest son, pointing his finger at me, as if to say, "I want you." A few weeks later, David explained that he was looking for his son. I asked David where he was. He said that his son was staying with his teacher and that she was taking care of him.

At that point, out of the clear blue, David asked if I would always be true to him. He called me "his wife." He asked, "Would you be the mother of my son?" He was talking about the son in the picture, whom I now assume was fictitious. I answered him that I could not be the mother to his son. "I have three sons," I said. I told David if his son needed help, I was in Boca for him. He could visit if he is down in Florida.

He then said, "Will you marry me?" I said "No! I will never marry anyone." Before Chuck died, he begged me to marry him and I had said no. I will never marry anyone again.

David started to call me "Babe." I told him that I was not his Babe and that I would never, ever be his Babe. I said that anyone else he was calling "Babe" who did not object to that phrase must be a prostitute. I felt a little bad about calling someone I did not know a prostitute, but that showed him how I detested the word.

David then sent me a list of names for me to select what I would like to be called. Something in the swiftness of his response turned me on. I think it was because I liked that he was trying to please me. Anyway, I chose the first name, Sunshine. He has called me that ever since.

David and I grew closer over time. At some point he told me he was a member of a United Nations team, as a traveling doctor who was stationed in different places. I was interested in how this worked. I asked him if he worked in dangerous areas. He said that he did and started to explain how he picked up wounded soldiers from the front lines, and then took them into physical safety back at his base. He spoke like he knew what he was talking about, and I believed him. I asked him how he stayed so calm in these dangerous situations. He said that doctors have to be calm. That statement turned my brain into a *Wow!* mode.

David promised me that he would meet me and that we would be together. He said he was in the United States and that he would see me soon. I was excited even though I didn't have any details. Then one day he sent me an email with four words: "I am in Iraq." I got upset and was in shock. I didn't know if he had always been in Iraq, or even whether he was really there now. But I was angry because just when I thought we might be close to meeting, he tells me he is on the other side of the globe. I was furious.

But our relationship continued. He continued with his line of compliments and even more advancements to me. David made me believe that he could and would do anything to get me. He continued to call me his wife, which in my mind was way out of line. He said he would get the boys to like him and to understand him and eventually to be proud to have him as a father. There was something about a determined man that I liked: someone who would take over or take care of a situation. I loved it when Chuck would take the reins, especially when there were major problems confronting us, and especially when it meant that the burden of responsibility could be shared. Maybe I needed a strong man because of something missing in my childhood with my father.

I never once saw David's face, though at the beginning he sent several different pictures of different men. But our email conversations got more personal, and we grew closer. He discussed having a future with his wife Brenda. I asked him to please stop saying that. "I am not your wife!" I repeated over and over again. "It bothers me when you say that." I asked him if he was crazy. He would get quiet and not answer. Once in a while he would tell me I would be his wife and he would take care of me forever.

We discussed the things we liked to do and life in general. I found out he likes to sleep on the right side of the bed. I said, "We can't get married because I sleep on the right side of the bed," even though I didn't have marriage in my head or heart. He replied, "We can work it out." Again, I liked his to-the-point short answers. But maybe they were somehow recorded or robot answers.

One day David emailed me and said, "Can you meet me on Hangout?" I said, "No—there is a Covid virus going around, and I am not leaving the house." That was a naive answer. He did not pay any attention to what I said. For about 15 emails he just kept telling me to go to Hangout—like it was a continuous robot message. I kept telling him that I would not leave the house, and I assumed that we had trouble communicating because his English was not perfect.

But then he added a few things to his sentence. "Go to Hangout, and you can see dogs, and my photos, and you can talk to me in private," he emailed me. I finally figured out that he was talking about Google Hangouts, the messaging app. I gave in and joined, since he was so insistent. Once I got the hang of Hangouts, I enjoyed getting to know David. He was more human, more loving, more caring, more inquisitive, and very interesting. We talked about a lot of things. He seemed to have a lot of time on his hands. It was almost as if we were together all day and night. That is when he sent a photo of him and five children—his one son multiplied five times.

I began to feel close to him. At some point he said that when he got his retirement pension, he wanted to rest, eat, and sleep, and for us to do things together. He loved books and wanted to read. Every word that came out of his mouth meant a lot to me.

I liked Hangouts because David seemed to always be available. Now I realize that if you are a scammer, you (or a group of people) are on the computer constantly. You (or they) are just a click away from scamming. As soon as I reached out to David on Hangouts, he would immediately pop up and say "I am here, I am here for you." I loved the simple sentence "I am here." That represented strength and someone to be there for me, in my mind. I liked the fact that I had someone to talk to whenever I wanted or needed to do so. And our conversations were fun.

Sadly for me, anytime David would do anything that made me happy, it did not last long. I wanted to share my happiness with my family and friends, but immediately I would get the same response. "He is not real," "he is a robot," "he is not a 'he' but a group of scammers from Africa," "he does not care about you," "he has many women he scams just like you," "you are just a number." At some level

I suspected they were right. But at another level, I was enjoying my time with David; it was exciting, and fun, and an adventure. And it helped relieve my loneliness.

Sometimes David had too much time on his hands and got carried away, forgetting what he had told me originally, and changing his story. Then I got a video he sent of him in Jerusalem from the past. He was walking down to the tomb of David, and said, "This is where David, my namesake, is buried. My room is just around the corner," he said, and then he climbed the stairs. It was all body shots from the back of him going toward the tomb and up the stairs. It turned out later that he had never been stationed in Jerusalem. He had forgotten that he had sent me that video. He was in over his head and was dealing with too many scams, I think. Still, I enjoyed our conversations.

All the time he spent with me was important during my alone period after Chuck had passed. I fell for David in a weird way. I really looked forward to our correspondence. He became more possessive and asked me questions about my feelings toward him, and he started calling me his "wife" more and more. I grew more and more entranced by him.

I told David one day that I had to run an errand. He asked if I had on makeup. I told him I did not use makeup—I think of foundation as makeup, and I don't use that. Anyway, I asked him why he cared. He said he did not want any men looking at me. I got quiet then and did not respond. David was different than any man I knew. He came up with things I had never heard from a man. He also asked if I would always be faithful to him, and if I would always be there for him. He called me his "beautiful wife," which blew me away.

After a while of texting each other back and forth, he seemed to get angry and asked why I never called him by his name, "David."

I never did. I had to ask myself why I never used his name. Maybe because there was no real face to attach a name to. His photos started changing when he would send me a photo. All I could think was that he had been doing the scamming for so long that he was not paying attention to what he was doing. Or he loved to play games with me constantly, which was rather frustrating.

Sometimes David went into detail about how the United Nations worked. I asked which countries he had been to as a United Nations traveling doctor. He started naming countries one after another. Argentina, England, all over the world. I asked him which he liked the best. Each country he named had an interesting story, and he would go into his spiel as always, which I loved.

He also started talking more about his situation in Iraq. I asked about how the women in the Middle East were treated, and he explained their role with men. At some point, he started to act very nervous. And then, out of the blue, he said he wanted to get out of Iraq and retire and be with me. I made the mistake of saying, "When are you going to do that?" He responded by saying that he needed the money to get to New York and start a new life. I asked why the United Nations wouldn't pay for it. He said they paid only for designated assignments, not for his retirement.

David then told me that I could pay for him to get out of Iraq. I was suspicious, but I also felt bad for him. He seemed scared. He said Iraq was stressful and dangerous. "I cannot take it here," he said, and he added that he desperately wanted to come to New York to collect his pension and retire. I eventually agreed to help.

David insisted that he needed cash to get out of Iraq. "Why can't you give me your flight information and I will buy the ticket on my credit card?" I asked. He said he could not use the credit card. I said

I could, knowing that I could hide the credit card number and buy the ticket personally. I insisted on using a credit card for about three or four days, until he lost his temper. This time, and every time I tried to use a credit card to help him with various things, he got very angry and accused me of not wanting to help him with retirement. It went back and forth until I thought he would have a nervous breakdown. He was 100% against me using my credit card and yelled at me, "I told you I don't want to talk about a credit card!" I now think that he probably wanted to avoid credit cards so that money would not be traceable to him. But I dropped the subject.

I agreed to send him cash. I went to the bank and withdrew several thousand dollars, all in hundred-dollar bills. I was very hesitant; I asked David several more times if I could just pay for the flight from Iraq on my credit card directly. He said no, and he began to lose patience with me. So, I got the cash, I got a FedEx box to put the money in, and I waited for David to call me with the correct address to send it to.

David had a friend in Texas who would be the point person for receiving the money and then sending it to David. David got the mailing address from the point person and made me repeat the address three times to make sure I got it right. He also gave me the point person's phone number and instructed me to text the point person the tracking number and delivery date as soon as I sent the package. I got the tracking number from Fed Ex, but, since the address was in a rural area, Fed Ex could only give me an approximate time for delivery. When I got this information, I texted it to the point person.

Once David got the money, he took a private plane from Iraq, supposedly to stay out of danger, and he sent a photo of himself on the plane, which I thought was authentic. It took almost a week to get to New York. He would occasionally call me on the way. He had a bad cold and we never had a good connection. If I asked a question, he would get quiet and then drop the call. He also had many layovers on his way to New York, and said he had to be tested for Covid at each stop. He seemed worn out. He said he was sleeping in the airport on his luggage, and that he needed to send one piece of luggage to China.

Once David got to New York, he asked me to switch from Hangouts to WhatsApp for our communication channel. I got an inexpensive phone and the WhatsApp app. On his WhatsApp page was the same picture he'd sent from the plane from Iraq. He told me, from that point on, that this photo of him was real. He later posted another picture on his WhatsApp page and kept it there. It had David about twenty yards in the distance in front of tall buildings in what seemed like New York City. He was nice looking. He had Caucasian skin and light brown hair and seemed about 60 years old. He was clean shaven with a nice haircut. He had a preppy look and wore a soft short-sleeved plaid shirt. I later asked David if his eyes were blue, but he said they were brown. I did not make a copy of his photo on the private jet, or from WhatsApp, so I do not have a photo of David.

Once we switched to WhatsApp, our relationship became very tiring for me. Things were not good and started going downhill. He was not as organized or responsive as he used to be. He said he was busy getting all of his papers filled out for his retirement from the United Nations. I also realized he liked expensive things. I once asked where he was staying in New York. He said he was staying at the Ritz Carlton. I was flabbergasted.

I didn't like communicating on WhatsApp. The connection was usually bad. And all sorts of strange things happened. I saw calls from David to Egypt, Georgia, and California. One time I saw a panoramic video of several Black men—for some reason I think they were Nigerian—in a small room. A few of them moved around the room. It lasted about five seconds and was shocking. It was not clear what they were saying. Later I heard a lawyer on my end talking to David about his U.N. pension and what he had to do to get it. The lawyer was also talking to David about a Supreme Court case that involved Chuck O'Brien. But it was not a case about my Chuck. As my son Jack told me, it was a case about flag burning involving someone else named O'Brien.

I confronted David with this. He was smart and asked me what I saw and heard. I asked him about the men, and how his Georgia peach was, and about his California girlfriend. He never really answered. He told me the lawyer's name but was misleading. I felt like I was on a merry-go-round. Once we switched to WhatsApp, David did not talk to me in a reliable way. I was getting very upset, and I let him know I did not like the WhatsApp conversations.

As time went on, the United Nations was requesting more information from him so that he could get his pension. Also, they charged him money to get his pension. I was getting frustrated and told him he needed to go to someone who could help him more with the process. As time went on, David seemed drugged. Whenever I called, we had a horrible connection. For some reason David would not call me; he instead asked that I call him. I finally said, "If you want to talk to me, you call me." He would pause for a short second and then say I needed to call him.

David made more mistakes. Out of the blue, a photo would show up of him, but it was not real. A day later he would ask that I delete the photo because it was not him and he said would get in trouble if he was caught using someone else's photo. Despite the fact that I knew he was bad, I still liked him. His personality made up for his mistakes.

David insisted that he would get me to marry him. I kept reminding him of our major age gap. He would try to explain that we were both grown-ups and that we had a life to plan together. He said, "Tell your sons I do not want your home—I will buy us a home, I will give you all that you have dreamed of." I told him I had all that I had dreamed of, and that I did not need a new home. Then he said: "I just don't want your boys to think I want to use you. I love you more than life, and I will take care of you for the rest of your life."

I told him he was getting caught in too many fabricated stories. He just went on with the marriage bit, that he would and could marry me. I kept telling him there was no way. This is when we started calling each other "stubborn." We decided that each of us were equally stubborn. We had a lot of fun times picking on each other—lots of laughter.

I was ready to receive David, and even though I knew when he was full of bull, and would tell him so, he told me in beautiful words that he loved me and would take care of me. And he asked me if I would be there for him. This bothered me. It was as if I was being confined again. I was back to my childhood, locked down with my mother, who constantly wanted me by her side.

One day he wrote, "Hey, Sunshine, I have good news from the United Nations: I will be getting paid, and I wish to make our meeting a memorable one. You are everything to me, and I can't do without you, my Sunshine. Loving you remains my top priority. I miss you so much and love you to the moon and back, my Sunshine." David always showered me with beautiful remarks just before he asked for money.

In the meantime, I would question him constantly—to the point I think I was driving him off the deep end. I would hear him go into a deep sigh—as if he were saying, "If she repeats herself one more time, I will scream." I asked if he was a robot as my children claimed, or if he was with a dangerous organization with sophisticated means to get me to agree to its wishes. He started laughing and said, "I am going to take a shower, and robots don't take showers." He would let me hear the shower water. David would always come out of the blue with a farfetched answer. If he was who the boys said he was, he must have been trained for years. He was an over-the-top pro.

One night I was sleeping, and at about three a.m. the phone rang; the connection was as clear as a bell. David started talking, and it went into a sexual phone call—the first one in my life, at age 80. He put the hook into me. You can imagine what I felt.

Eventually I sent money to David to help him process his U.N. papers. I sent it with the same cash system, but I sent it to someone in Connecticut. It arrived in New York a few days later, I was told. I don't know if this was a scam. But I didn't care.

About six or so times David said he would come see me in Boca Raton. He would say he would see me "tomorrow," or "next week," or "soon." I told him that he could not get to my home because there was a security gate. David threatened violence, as he often did in our conversations. He said, "I will shoot my way through." He said he would show up at my door in the middle of the night. Then with each crazy violent threat, he would laugh.

Every time David said he would see me, I hoped he would follow through. He never did. I waited for him every time, and he always had excuses. One excuse after he left New York was that he was on the way to see me and had flown into the Ft. Lauderdale airport (which is close to my home in Boca Raton) but had caught Covid on the airplane and was being held in Ft. Lauderdale airport. I told him I could come down to Ft. Lauderdale to see what was going on.

He said no, he could handle it. He then sent me a copy of what was supposed to be his Covid positive test. It was a counterfeit.

Soon I got a call from David, who said I needed to talk to his doctor, Dr. Roberts. He told me David was in bad shape and needed a special Covid medicine from Greece. He told me David needed $20,000 to get his medicine right away. I told Dr. Roberts I could not do that. I also told him David was not my husband and that he was responsible for his own medical needs. Dr. Roberts accused me of being cold and non-caring. I replied that I am not responsible for David's life. Dr. Roberts called me cruel. I told him Remdesivir had cured a family friend and her husband, and I recommended he get that, since it was available in the United States. I then spoke to David. He sounded very sick. I repeated to him what I told the doctor about Remdesivir.

The next day David was moved from Ft Lauderdale to a Carrolton, Texas, hospital. Carrolton was near where his friend, the money conduit, lived. He told me he was doing a bit better, but he sounded horrible, as if his lungs were failing. I told him to rest and do whatever the doctors recommended.

As the days progressed, he started sounding a bit better. I asked what was the latest from the United Nations. He broke down and said that the U.N. was dragging its feet on getting him his pension because of Covid. I told him to go to the top of the United Nations to get answers. I asked him if he wanted me to talk to my son Jack on how he could expedite his pension. He soon started crying and said, "All I have is you, Brenda, and Jack." I wondered why he thought Jack was on his side, since I had only asked whether he wanted me to ask Jack for help. This, of course, made me feel sorry for David.

I twice more sent money to David in Texas to help him. The first time, David told me that the money was being delivered to him by a boy on a motorcycle who was hit by a truck and killed, and the money was never found. The second time, David told me the woman who was delivering the money was robbed as she left her home.

I worried that if the cops found the money from the motorcycle, I would get in trouble since my return address was on the box. But I also suspected a scam. My mother had experienced something similar. She had sent her maid Cora to the racetrack to bet, and Mother won around two thousand dollars. When Cora came home, she told Mother there was an accident on the bridge, and when she got out of the car to see what was going on, someone stole the money. So I did not really believe either of David's stories.

From this point on our relationship really deteriorated. I was starting to realize that David was a scam, and my boys were pressuring me to end the relationship. When I suggested to David that I might end the relationship, he threatened to kill himself. During our year of conversations, he said he would kill himself at least three times, and each time he said he would put my name on it. I told David that, if he killed himself, I would not be responsible and that, if he put my name on it, that would be horrible. He said he only meant to suggest that he would miss me.

By January 2021, my boys insisted that I put David in my past and start a new life. On New Year's Eve, I had hoped to see David. He did not come. (The next day I told him, "New Year's came and went without you.") I decided to have a New Year's Eve meal at a local restaurant. As I was leaving the restaurant my right knee gave out, and I fell and hurt my knee very badly and had to go to the emergency room. The knee would take three months to heal.

My boys viewed my New Year's Eve accident as the last straw with David, since they thought I was communicating with him when I fell. Soon after the accident, they suggested they might put me in to a financial receivership to keep me from paying money to David, and they threatened to cut off my communications with him. This angered me. I thought: *Shame on them—I don't give a damn.* It seemed strange that I was at a point in my life of wanting to be in a receiving situation, and yet my boys were interfering. The circumstances and odds were against me.

I eventually agreed to let my boys take my computer and phone and retire them to the burial grounds. My new phone number had a Philadelphia area code and was so hard to remember that I still do not know it. I have had to adjust and listen to my boys' demands.

I know that the boys were probably right that David was a scam artist. But I did have feelings for him that I had never had in my life. I did let him go, but it was not a decision for me, it was a decision for my boys. They kept telling me that I was in danger with his lies, deception, and manipulation. I know that I was in need because the love of my life, Chuck, was gone. David was filling a void that I needed so badly to be filled—especially during the loneliness of Covid.

It really hurt to let him go, but that is life. I had a relationship with him that I have never had in my life. My boys love me and care that I don't get hurt. But I pray if the time does come and he reaches out, they will listen to his story. There is so much they do not know; they only surmise. There is a major human side to David, the Academy Award actor. If he was sad, I could tell. If I picked him up, I could tell. If he was worried or had fear or love, I could tell. If I aggravated him, I could tell. Can you imagine talking to someone whose face you've never really seen—and yet you really know him? If David is 100% a con artist, I did not see or feel all 100%. He was several people, and I saw each side of him, including some disturbing sides. Again, all my loved ones and friends would say none of it was real.

I do not have a copy of the last letter I sent directly to David. The bottom line was that I told David our relationship was coming to an end and that all communication would end. I sent him the lyrics of *The Winner Takes It All*, by ABBA. This song is the number-one breakup song of all time, and I used it to make it final with David. Here are the first two stanzas:

> *I don't wanna talk*
> *About things we've gone through*
> *Though it's hurting me*
> *Now it's history*
>
> *I've played all my cards*
> *And that's what you've done, too*
> *Nothing more to say*
> *No more aces to play*

When you face closure, you have to accept that it is over. I told David he had to do three things to get our life worked out and to get us back together. First, he had to give me my money back. Second, he had to talk to all three of my sons. Third, he had to give up his life as it is now. It is hard to care for someone and not be able to know who they are. It is a strange feeling, not trusting and yet loving and caring for someone. This experience is all new for me, and I am trying to work through it with my head on straight.

The following email came from David on Jan. 8, 2021.

> *Hi. Thanks for your response. I wish to reaffirm my position that I can't close our relationship because you still have the whole*

of my heart. I can't and will never forget you, my Sunshine.
Please try to get your WhatsApp sorted and resolved ASAP. I
have missed you so much, my beautiful wife. I love you. David.

David also later wrote the following:

1. *Baby, I really want you to get me an Amazon card. In time, I*
   will speak to you when I am not busy. I can send you back your
   money so just try and get me the Amazon on time so I can send
   you your money on time.

2. *Baby, just forget about yourself. You can't just believe what your son*
   is telling you. We are both together on this, I swear. I did not have
   sufficient money; I really want to use the Amazon card to subscribe or
   unsubscribe, and I will send you the money. I want you to believe me.
   Don't be afraid, okay? People may say anything to square us apart,
   but the most important thing is that you have to just get the Amazon
   card $200, so I can describe the network and send you back your
   money. If you believe me and get the Amazon card, you will see what
   I am talking about. You will receive your money back in 3 hours.

3. *Baby, I really want you to get the Amazon card. Forget about*
   what your son says. I am real, and I am truthful to what I said.
   Just get me the Amazon card $200 so I can subscribe my network.
   That is the only way I can get you the money. Get me the Amazon
   card and your bank number, so I can send you the money. You
   will receive it in less than one hour. Don't listen to what your son
   is talking about—he is just a kid.

Why he used "baby," I don't know—when he knew how much
I hated "Babe," and this was just too close to "Babe." I think he just

wanted my bank account number, which I am sure would have been a coup for him. I would never be that naïve.

Later I sent another letter to David, though my son Brett sent it from a fake account to protect me. I needed to let him know that I was not sending any more money and that he knew my address and could send the money by postal service. Even though I was truly seeking closure with my last letter, I had to get it off my chest that he had done nothing for me. He had truly been a scammer. Here is what the letter said:

Hi, David,

As you know, the last email was meant to put an end to our relationship—in other words, closure. Just so you know, instead of thinking about David, I'm thinking of Brenda now. You told me not to think about Brenda. If I don't think about Brenda, who will, David?

If you got your money from the United Nations, why do you need more money in a credit card form of $200.00? I have no idea, but there will be no more money from myself. I gave you my heart, soul, and money, and you gave me zero. Absolutely zero that you promised for one year. Just go back and think of all the future things you promised for the two of us. You will continue to get zero from me for the rest of my life, so don't waste your time on telling me how great our life will be together, so you can get more money from me. Unfortunately, I hope you do not use those lines on an innocent woman.

You did not show up for Christmas, but you did send chocolate kisses that I found out just recently were charged to my Amazon account. So again, my happiness was stripped away by your scam. Also, you broke my heart when you said to trash your Christmas gifts that I still have, because you were mad that I did not send you more money and said I could not send you any more money. You were supposed to show up for my birthday and never did. When Valentine's Day came, I looked outside the door, thinking I would get something from you, but, of course, there was nothing.

The very last conversation before I cut off communication with you was that you were coming to my home, we would have a memorable time together, and that there would be no closure from you, as I had the "whole of your heart forever." I listened for the doorbell for three weeks—and no David. I had asked that you come on Saturday or Sunday as no one would be here; I asked you not to come on Friday at 10:00. I also told the gate you would be coming—but no David.

This is why our relationship, or whatever we had going on, is over.

I found it strange that you did not say, "Brenda I know your address, and I will get the money to you as promised" in the last email that you sent. There is such a thing as the postal service, and I can sign for the envelope, or you could just come by and hand me the envelope in person.

IF YOU WERE ANY KIND OF A MAN with good intentions, you would take the initiative to take the steps to work out the things you need to and get me my money without—for heaven's sake!—asking me for more money to help you get me my money. Another horrible disappointment, David.

I can only think of how many times I went out of my way to make sure that I took care of you. Will you do the same and go out of your way, as I did, to take care of Brenda?

Whatever you are doing, I hope it is legit and a good lifestyle and not every day and every second of every day ruining the lives of women.

My best to you David,

Brenda

In reflecting on my experience with David, I have—as this chapter makes clear—deeply mixed emotions. I know that David made his most loving statements just before he wanted, and sometimes demanded, money from me. I was upset at times about what David did to me. But David also served an important role in my life during the difficult, sad, lonely year of Covid, just after Chuck passed. I don't feel bad about my actions. I acted and reacted as I had all of my life—simply as myself. If I were someone else, I could have walked away. But that would not have been me.

Perhaps not surprisingly, the experience with David mirrored many elements of my life. For example, he often talked and threatened violence. This took me back to my father's drinking days. David finagled money out of me. My Aunt Opal sometimes stole from my mother, yet Mother knew all the time what was going on but never scolded my aunt, simply because she was a loving and giving person. David tried to be manipulative. This reminded me of my brother Louis Jack's many manipulations and mind games.

In short, each day with David was another trip down memory lane. But it was a fresh trip, one that captured my attention and relieved some of my loneliness. I believed that David, real or not, needed me—and I needed him. I will never apologize for my actions with David. I knew what I was doing, and I was in control.

Divine Intervention and Timing

My life has been aided by divine intervention and timing. Every time I was on my last leg—which was more than a few times!—God intervened to help me. If someone was missing in my life, someone else showed up. If I was confused, a friend would help. Whenever something bad happened to me, divine intervention led things in a better direction.

Jack Jr. helped me to escape from feeling choked and suffocated in West Memphis. He did not always treat me well. But he gave to me the most precious and wonderful sons a mother could ever wish for.

Bob Rivet arrived after Jack Jr. left us, and he took care of me and my boys in a lovely home in a beautiful neighborhood with good schools. Bob and I did not always get along, but he did give us love and helped us all at a hard time.

Chuck, too, appeared during a low time in our lives. He gave me and the boys undying love, took care of us, and protected us, even though he brought the Hoffa ordeal into our family.

I underwent shock treatments at one of the low points in my life. Thank goodness for the shock treatments. Everyone around me thought they were gruesome, but they got me through the rest of my life with so much calm and confidence, helping me to believe in myself and know who I was.

And more than anything else, I always had music. Music soothed my soul when I was a little girl, and it helped me through every difficult stage of my life.

As I wrote this book, I wondered how I got through so many things and kept going. My son Jack says that I am resilient. Resilience is the capacity to recover and regain happiness from difficult situations. I do think I am resilient. I believe.

Acknowledgments

For support on this book, and in my life, I thank my beautiful family, Chuck's beautiful family, Floyd Newman, Boo Mitchell, Charles and Clay Calello, Pam Tillis and Matt Spicher, Molly Secours, Kojo Hayes, Adjowa Hayes, Nina Giacalone, Captain Bill Lepree, Tim Sampson, Toni Wiley, Tarsia Smith, Zoila Ramirez, Kris Thomas, Tim and Pam Wallace, Tim Kuhlman, Dr. Karin Holden-Alfaro, Steven Bercovitch, Rita Fulginiti, Rob Roy, Paul Kronk, Shayne Leighton, Michael Kraft, Rod Cortizo, Kirill Hitroff, Mark and Shona Hudson, Linzey Rose, Greg Gregory, Rick Krive, Marcos Dacosta, Michael Jon, Senator Keith Ingram, and Caesar Brown.

About the Author

B renda O'Brien is a mother, songwriter, music producer, philanthropist, and the longtime President of Pancho's Mexican Restaurant in Memphis, Tennessee. Brenda's best-known song is "Two Kings," sung by Pam Tillis and Kris Thomas, and "Remember," an anti-bullying anthem. Brenda grew up in the heart of the honky tonks, truck stops and nightclubs of West Memphis, Arkansas. Her family ran the famous Plantation Inn, which saw regular performances by dozens of the rock and roll and blues greats in the mid-South in the 1940s and 1950s, many of which Brenda knew from a young age.